Nancy Love
WASP PILOT

Nancy Harkness Love, WAFS founder, Senior Squadron Leader; Executive for WAFS, Executive for WASP of the Ferrying Division, Air Transport Command. *Courtesy: WASP Archive, TWU Libraries' Women's Collection, Texas Woman's University, Denton, Texas.*

Nancy Love
WASP PILOT

by Sarah Byrn Rickman

FILTER PRESS, LLC
Palmer Lake, Colorado

ISBN: 978-0-86541-255-2
Library of Congress Control Number: 2018966885

Copyright © 2019 Sarah Byrn Rickman. All Rights Reserved.

This Filter Press publication is a Young Adult edition of *Nancy Love and the WASP Ferry Pilots of World War II* (University of North Texas Press, copyright 2008 Sarah Byrn Rickman), by permission of UNT Press.

Cover image used courtesy the WASP Archive, Texas Woman's University, Denton.
Cover & Interior design by Robert Schram, Bookends Design

Published by Filter Press, LLC, Palmer Lake, CO 80133
No part of this book may be mechanically or electronically reproduced without written permission of the publisher. For information, contact Filter Press at 888.570.2663 or info@FilterPressBooks.com.

Manufactured in the United States of America

Dedication

This book is dedicated to original WAFS Nancy Batson Crews, the twentieth woman pilot accepted to fly for the Ferrying Division, Air Transport Command in WWII. She was my mentor, my inspiration, my collaborator on my first book, *The Originals*, and my friend. Without her, I would never have known the incredible story of Nancy Love and her women pilots. And none of my now nine books about the WASP would exist.

Contents

Prologue	ix
One: Nice Young Ladies	1
Two: NOT Love at First Sight	7
Three: Flight Testing the Safety Planes	13
Four: WAR!	21
Five: Enter: The WAFS	27
Six: Cochran Comes Home	33
Seven: A Study in Contrasts	39
Eight: The Originals Gather	43
Nine: Growing Pains	51
Ten: The WAFS Lose One	61
Eleven: Transport and Transition	65
Twelve: A B-17 Bound for England	75
Thirteen: Trouble Brewing	81
Fourteen: WASP Will Fly Pursuit	85
Fifteen: Pursuit School	93
Sixteen: The Quest for Militarization	99
Seventeen: The Women in Pursuit	107
Eighteen: Officer Training School	113
Nineteen: Militarization Denied	117
Twenty: Tunner Is Transferred	121
Twenty-one: Closing Down	127

Twenty-two: Nancy Flies the Big One	133
Twenty-three: The Hump	137
Epilogue	145
Flying High	149
Airplanes Flown by Nancy Love	155
Awards and Honors	158
Glossary and Acronyms	159
Timeline	161
Bibliography	164
Acknowledgments	170
About the Author	171
Also by Sarah Byrn Rickman	172

Prologue

THE ARMY C-54 BEGAN ITS TAKEOFF ROLL. The lumbering giant strained to gain momentum. The wind caught its wings, and the aircraft lifted from the runway.

Fully loaded, the four-engine wartime beast of burden climbed up through the heavy humid air of Calcutta, India. The pilot set an east-by-northeast heading and flew out over the jungles of east India.

The aircraft was headed to "The Hump"—a World War II highway in the sky over the Himalayan Mountains and the impenetrable jungles of Burma. This was the United States' all-important wartime supply route to war-weary Kunming, China.

A woman's hands held the controls of the 38,930-pound cargo/transport plane. The pilot's name was Nancy Harkness Love.

In spite of the airplane's size, power and heft, hydraulics (water under pressure that made the airplane easier to handle) assured that a woman could fly it as well as a man. At five-feet-six and blessed with long legs, Nancy was tall enough for her feet to comfortably reach the rudders.

The familiar throb of the four engines soon calmed the adrenalin high triggered by her first trip over the rooftop of the world.

The date was January 8, 1945. World War II had entered its final year. Victory would come first in Germany with the Allied countries' defeat of the Nazis in May. Japan would surrender in August.

But it wasn't over yet.

✣ ✣ ✣

After landing in Kunming, Nancy parked the airplane, cut the switches, and cleaned up the cockpit. She rose, dropped her headset on the seat, and followed her passengers and crew out of the airplane into the cold dry air and pale winter sunshine. She wore a wrinkled khaki Army-issue flight suit and bulky leather jacket. But for her softly waved, chin-length hair, she might have passed for a young male crewman.

As she walked toward the group of officers clustered on the ground, she did not stride purposefully, nor did she walk like many women would have, to call attention to herself. She was, in fact, slightly pigeon-toed and had a hint of a glide to her step. She moved with a poise that conveyed more self-assurance than she actually felt. She extended her hand and offered a firm handshake.

Always guarded, Nancy didn't try to impress. She stayed low-key. When she smiled, her luminous, gold-flecked hazel eyes took in each man, graciously making him feel as if he was the object of that smile.

Thirty-year-old Nancy Love was a strikingly beautiful woman with high cheekbones and delicate features. Her light brown hair had begun to go gray at nineteen, beginning with a streak that swept back from the right side of her forehead. The gray gave her an aura of maturity.

Her reserve, carefully honed over those thirty years, masked her drive. Nancy greeted challenges with cool assessment, never allowing the passion that lurked beneath the surface to show in her soft voice. That she had been asked to take part in this flight, to fly this airplane, was a coup, the high point in a distinguished aviation career that, by 1945, had covered fifteen years.

Dutifully, she recorded the Hump flight in her logbook. [Pilots keep a record of all their flights in a logbook.] She wrote nothing else of the flight. She didn't need to. She had done it. She was the first woman to pilot a military airplane over the Hump.

Nancy Love in Army issue coveralls with a parachute over her shoulders.
Courtesy: Author's Personal Collection, gift of Nancy Batson Crews.

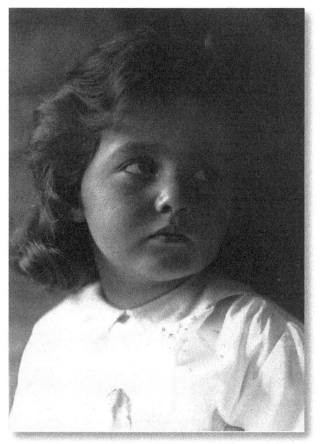

Hannah Lincoln "Nancy" Harkness, age three. *Courtesy: The Love family collection.*

Chapter One

Nice Young Ladies

"NICE YOUNG LADIES DON'T DO SUCH THINGS," Nancy's mother said when her daughter announced she'd like to learn to fly. Sixteen-year-old Hannah Lincoln Harkness—born Valentine's Day in 1914 and nicknamed Nancy by her father—had seen a barnstormer pilot performing loops and rolls over her Houghton, Michigan, home. The little airplane seemed to dance in the sun, catching and reflecting the rays off its yellow wings.

For a penny a pound, a dollar and change at her weight, Nancy wangled a ride with 18-year-old pilot Jimmy Hansen.

A 360-degree roll left and one to the right were followed by some over-and-under loops that were stock thrills that traveling pilots, like Jimmy, executed for first-timers. If Jimmy thought these would turn this young lady green, he was wrong.

She was hooked and said so that evening at the dinner table.

"Daddy, I want to learn to fly." Flying, she added, was far more fun than school. She intended to give all her time to flying.

Dr. Robert Bruce Harkness hid his amusement. He adopted a stern face and worked out a deal with her. Yes, she could take flying lessons, but school was not optional. She would return to Milton Academy, a prep school outside Boston, in the fall.

When she left for her first flying lesson, her father told her, "Do it well or not at all." For the rest of his life, Dr. Harkness kept a scrapbook of his precocious daughter's aviation exploits. Throughout the rest of her life, Nancy followed those seven words of advice from her father.

She soloed—flew alone in the airplane—after only four hours, thirty minutes flying time in Jimmy's Fleet Biplane. Before long she had earned her private pilot's license.

Back at school in Boston, she didn't waste any time getting in the air.

> I was still just sixteen when I took off on my first cross-country—from Boston to Poughkeepsie. I had two friends along and all our luggage.
>
> We were on our way from Milton to Vassar College to visit friends. The ship was far too large and complicated for my fifteen solo hours. Once in the air, I realized I had never used an aircraft compass before. I couldn't read it!
>
> Our luggage was in the right seat beside me. My two passengers were sitting in the back. They had no idea how inadequate and frightened I suddenly felt.
>
> I noticed ugly clouds coming from the west and they were moving fast. I couldn't really see that well. I flew lower and lower in an effort to see out. With that, the oil gauge broke and smeared black stuff all over the windscreen. That meant I had no visibility at all to the front.
>
> I had to hang my head out the open side window. My inflamed imagination convinced me the motor was about to stop. I picked out a field that looked smooth—it was winter, so not much vegetation—and I landed. Lucky for me and my passengers, we and the ship were still intact.
>
> It taught me a great deal in a short time, and ended happily, but due to age and inexperience seemed tenser than any later experience.

Nancy Harkness, age 16. *Courtesy: The Love family collection.*

Her second close call wasn't long in coming.

Flying with her one Sunday, her brother Bob dared her to buzz the boys' prep school near Milton. She flew low down the quadrangle and tried to pull up at the far end to avoid hitting the chapel.

Nancy still hadn't learned the laws of physics. She didn't realize that though you pull back on the control stick, the plane doesn't immediately go up. She nearly hit the top of the building, rattling roof slates in the process.

Someone got the tail number of the airplane.

Two local boys, the Fuller brothers, were known for such stunts. The irate headmaster of the boys' academy rang the airport manager. "Which one of those Fuller boys just buzzed the school?" and he gave the tail number identifying the plane.

The manager answered that the pilot of the plane was Miss Nancy Harkness.

Bob drove her back to school. When she walked into her residence hall, the headmistress, the housemistress, and two members of the board of trustees were waiting for her. Her brother took one look and bolted, leaving her to explain.

Nancy wasn't suspended. The school had no rules about flying. Students couldn't drive cars, but nothing said they couldn't fly airplanes. She was severely reprimanded and told to stay out of airplanes for the remainder of the semester.

✈ ✈ ✈

Contrary to her mother's warning, it turned out that nice young ladies did fly. That fall Nancy entered Vassar College in Poughkeepsie, New York. There, she organized a student-flying club. When asked, she organized flying clubs for other schools that made up the Seven Sisters, as those exclusive women's colleges in the northeast were called.

Nancy earned her limited commercial license in 1932 and her transport license the summer of 1933. She was not yet twenty.

The Great Depression, a long-lasting economic downturn that brought about bank failures, a decline in industrial output, and job loss, affected the lives of all Americans. In the Harkness family, the

Depression meant that Nancy did not return to Vassar in January 1934. She had to go to work when all she wanted to do was fly.

A wealthy uncle, her mother's brother Thomas L. Chadbourne, came to the rescue. To help Nancy become "employable," he paid for her to attend secretarial school in New York. Uncle Tom also let her live in his apartment rent-free. She invited two other young women flyers, Margaret (Tommy) Thomas and Suzanne Humphries, to move in with her.

Uncle Tom's apartment had once been the residence of famous American author Mark Twain. The address was 21 Fifth Avenue at the corner of Ninth Street, just down from Washington Square and on the edge of Greenwich Village. By the time the three girls lived there, the three-story brick house had been divided into apartments.

In her 1993 book, *Taking Off*, Margaret Thomas Warren wrote about the time she spent in New York with Nancy and Suzanne. "We were three young fliers. Good-looking, penniless and out to seek our fortunes. We were about the same age and our common burning interest, no, our passion, was flying."

Years later, Nancy delighted in telling her three daughters about her New York days. "I was so poor, I lived on tomato soup."

"Sometimes we actually missed a meal or so," Tommy wrote, "but we did have a steady supply of beer because somebody whose father owned a brewery sent it—like a standing order for roses to a chorus girl. We also had a constant supply of male friends and never lacked invitations out to meals. There were plenty, but pilots mostly—not a rich lot."

Most conversations among the three were about flying. One night, Tommy relates, "we all got in about the same time, very late, from our dates and nightclub visits. We talked awhile and then decided to go to Roosevelt Field [on nearby Long Island] and fly as soon as the sun was up.

Nancy Harkness and a Great Lakes trainer. *Courtesy: WASP Archive, Texas Woman's University, Denton.*

"Flying made women comrades in the same way that men can be comrades, but women seldom are. There are many ties women share, woman-to-woman, to men's exclusion, but we are rarely companions in the 'Three Musketeers' sense."

The living arrangement lasted but a few months. Nancy found secretarial school impossibly boring and decided to return to Boston to look for a job in aviation and live with her mother's family there.

Her friend and fellow pilot Henry Wilder accompanied Nancy on her job search. He suggested that they go see Bob Love at East Boston Airport. Bob might just know of something.

Chapter Two

NOT Love at First Sight

BOB LOVE WAS FIVE-FEET, ELEVEN-INCHES TALL with sandy red hair, a broad nose, and a wry sense of humor. He owned Inter City Aviation, a flight service out of East Boston.

Bob had attended Princeton and the Massachusetts Institute of Technology, but aviation so distracted him that he never finished college.

With financial help from his older sister, in 1932 he founded Inter City Aviation to offer instruction, charter flights, aerial surveying, and an unscheduled passenger service. He also sold airplanes and earned commissions from the aircraft manufacturers.

When Nancy and Henry arrived at the ICA office, Bob was away picking up an airplane.

Henry ushered Nancy into Bob's office, deposited himself in Bob's chair, and put his feet up on Bob's desk. Nancy boosted herself onto the desk, crossed her legs, and picked up her conversation with Henry.

Fifteen minutes later, the door banged open, and a man in grease-stained flight coveralls strode in.

A leather flight helmet and goggles dangled by their straps from one hand. He ran his other hand through his hair, mashed flat by the leather helmet. His cheeks were wind-burned. Blue eyes looked

Robert MacClure Love. *Courtesy: The Love family collection.*

out from raccoon-like white circles, the result of wearing goggles while flying an open cockpit airplane.

He took in the scene in one glance. Perched on *his* desk in *his* office, obviously in deep conversation with *his* friend Henry Wilder, was a beautiful young woman. She glanced up and smiled when he walked in, but she made no move to get off the desk.

Bob ordered his friend out of his chair and the woman off his desk.

For Nancy, a chance to be around airplanes all day everyday was what that awful stint in secretarial school and all that tomato soup had been about. Now this rude man had the nerve to order her around like some junior flunky.

She slid gracefully from the desk, shot him a withering look, and, mustering all her dignity, walked from the room. She slammed the door, leaving Henry to do the explaining.

In 1934, Nancy Harkness went to work for Bob Love at Inter City Aviation. *Courtesy: The Love family collection.*

Henry came out, looking sheepish, and asked her to come back in the office. Bob Love, disagreeable as he had sounded, really did want to meet her.

Nancy desperately wanted a job in aviation. She had come here to meet this Bob Love person. Why pass up the opportunity? Just because he was testy, didn't mean she had to be. She took a deep breath and nodded at Henry. He held the door for her as she re-entered the ogre's office.

Bob Love hired the attractive Miss Harkness. Not long after, an article appeared in *New England Aviation* headlined "Woman Flier Given Praise . . . To Demonstrate Waco Line." [The aircraft manufacturer Weaver Aircraft Company of Ohio is best known by the initials W-A-C-O.]

"She's OK. She's not just somebody that flies," Bob Love was quoted as saying. The article went on to say that:

Miss Harkness is a transport pilot and in the future will demonstrate the Waco line of airplanes to prospective customers. She has been flying for four years. . . . She is quite reserved but like all pilots warms up to the topic of flying so eventually some of her past experiences come to light. . . . It is anticipated that when this latest employee of the ICA becomes a little better acquainted she is going to be more than busy with her gray demonstrator which by the way is the only ambulance plane in New England.

Her job with Bob was demonstrating and selling airplanes on commission. She earned money each time she sold a plane. She was also the airport "Girl Friday," or all-purpose assistant.

On September 10, an article appeared in the Houghton, Michigan, newspaper stating that pilot Robert Love of Boston, Massachusetts, and well-known local aviatrix Miss Nancy Harkness, daughter of Dr. and Mrs. R. B. Harkness, had flown into the local airport in a Waco cabin plane. Nancy was taking Bob home to meet Mother and Daddy.

By early 1935, changes were in the air. Two well-known women pilots, Phoebe Omlie and Louise Thaden, with timely support from the world's most famous aviatrix, Amelia Earhart, had convinced the chief of the Airport Marking and Mapping Section of the Bureau of Air Commerce that towns and cities needed to be easily identifiable from the air.

There were no established airways—designated highways in the sky—like we have today. Planes didn't have radios. Getting lost was frighteningly easy, even for an experienced pilot.

Omlie's solution was to mark off each state in sections of twenty square miles, paint the name of the town on the roof of the most prominent building, and place markers at 15-mile intervals between towns. She and Thaden built the project from scratch.

Then they hired two rising young stars among the available female flyers, Nancy Harkness of Boston and Helen MacCloskey of Pittsburgh, to share the workload.

Going to work for the well-known and respected women flyers Thaden and Omlie meant leaving Inter City Aviation and Bob, but it was a big boost for Nancy's aviation career.

Omlie returned to her job with the Bureau of Air Commerce. Louise, Nancy, and Helen's job was to convince town leaders to hire out-of-work men to paint the signs.

Nancy's first day at work was September 14, 1935.

Soon after, an interview with Nancy appeared in the *Boston Post*. She told the reporter, "I love it. It's really useful work in the field of aviation and I get lots of chances to fly. Two other girls have similar jobs. . . . I have from Maine to Florida and Michigan and Ohio."

The article went on to say:

> But Miss Harkness, who is barely over 20—and very pretty—can smile wisely to herself. For now she wears a sizable and very sparkling diamond ring on her left hand and she is engaged to the president of Inter City Airlines, Robert Love, son of a New York banker.

Nancy Love was twenty-two when she fulfilled the requirements for the prestigious Fédération Aéronautique Internationale license, as attested by the National Aeronautic Association of the United States, on September 21, 1936. *Courtesy: The Love family collection.*

Chapter Three

Flight Testing the Safety Planes

NANCY KNEW AND FLEW with many of the male aviators in the 1930s. Aviation, then, was a small close-knit community. By 1935, she was on first name basis with U.S. Department of Air Commerce's Eugene Vidal and Bureau of Air Commerce's John Wynne.

Bob Love was from the Midwest and down to earth. That set him apart from the eligible males of the Eastern social set and most of the generation's "flyboys." Spirit of adventure aside, from the beginning he was a businessman and a good one, not a man given to a life of leisure.

"Laugh crinkles set off his glacial blue eyes," his daughter Hannah recalled.

"Mum called him homely-handsome," says daughter Marky. "He was very attractive to women."

Bob was completely at home with himself. He was as open and outgoing as Nancy was guarded and reserved. He was like no one Nancy had ever known. Likewise, she was completely unlike any girl he had ever met.

After that first shaky encounter in his office, things smoothed out, but their daughters never learned how long it took before the air between them thawed. But, January 11, 1936, Hannah Lincoln (Nancy) Harkness became the bride of Robert MacLure Love in

Nancy Love (second from left) and Betty Huyler Gillies (second from right) and friends at Roosevelt Field, Long Island. *Courtesy: The Air Power Museum, Farmingdale, Long Island.*

the First Presbyterian Church of Hastings, Michigan. Nancy's parents had recently moved from Houghton in Michigan's Upper Peninsula to Hastings in Michigan's Lower Peninsula.

✣ ✣ ✣

The honeymoon over, Nancy and Bob settled down outside of Boston. Nancy was content to continue flying demos and giving rides to passengers. Like most new brides in the mid-1930s, she expected to be pregnant before the year was out. For Nancy and Bob, that didn't happen.

The reluctance to call attention to herself manifested itself in many ways: her aversion to the limelight and publicity and the dislike of being photographed. Yet, Nancy was considered good copy by the Boston newspapers. Whatever she did drew attention from the press. The *Boston Traveler* wrote: "Her taxi is the 'Hammond Y,'

Nancy Love and the Stearman-Hammond Y aircraft, 1937. *Courtesy: The Love family collection.*

winner of the design competition of the Department of Commerce. She cruises at about 95 miles an hour and can go at 112; and she stops within 100 feet after she touches ground."

✢ ✢ ✢

"She was physically aware of herself—and yet uninterested in clothes, makeup, the trappings of the world of beauty and fashion," her daughter Allie said. "She wanted to be physically attractive to men, but she was not a flirt. Dignity was very important to her."

As 1937 dawned, Nancy's aviation career took yet another turn. She was offered the job of testing a new "safety plane" for the Bureau of Air Commerce. The new plane had a tricycle landing gear, that is, one wheel in the front and the two main wheels behind. Until the late 1930s, all airplanes were 'taildraggers' with the main wheels under the wings and a very small wheel in the tail.

The angle at which a taildragger airplane sat on the ground made it difficult for the pilot to see over the engine. The bigger the engine, the less forward visibility. When taxiing a taildragger on the ground, the pilot must "S"—or zigzag—in order to see what is in front of her.

March 9, 1937, Nancy recorded her last Hammond Y flight in her logbook. She resumed working with Bob at Inter City where her reputation as a competent pilot continued to grow.

That summer, Bob asked her to fly a Paramount News film crew to the local yacht races. At first the men were dubious about flying with a woman. But she zoomed them in low and slow where they could get all the great shots they wanted.

When they returned to East Boston late that afternoon, the windblown, flush-faced men had nothing but praise for the lady pilot. That put a very broad grin on the face of one Robert M. Love.

On August 30, 1937, Nancy got her second crack at an aircraft with the revolutionary tricycle landing gear. She made her first flight in the Gwinn Aircar in Buffalo, New York. The Gwinn Aircar was a stubby little aircraft designed by Joseph Marr Gwinn Jr., whose goal was to build an airplane that would replace the family automobile.

Nancy Love was not Gwinn's first choice for test pilot. Frank Hawks, a World War I flight instructor and barnstormer, dubbed the king of speed and aviation daring, was Gwinn's first choice, but Hawks had been called to Hollywood. Nancy was available. She had logged nearly sixty hours on the Hammond Y. And, she had more than 500 hours total flying time. Joe Gwinn hired her, and they went to work.

In flight, Joe sat in the right seat of the two-place aircraft, making mental engineering calculations and working them out with a slide rule. Nancy sat on the left in the pilot's seat at the controls.

Nancy Love stepping from the Gwinn Aircar, 1938. *Courtesy: The Love family collection.*

Joe wanted to land the plane from an altitude of 2,000 feet with the control column pulled full back, flaps down, and engine throttled. This violated every flying instinct Nancy possessed. Nancy was a perfectionist, as her approach to flying revealed. She ignored her pilot's instinct to push the nose down, which would have spoiled the test, she gritted her teeth and did what he asked. It worked!

Nancy became enamored of the strange-looking little craft and, as the Gwinn Aircar moved closer to reality, she believed a family aircraft was the wave of the future and promoted it.

Public relations whiz Harry Bruno was working on the Aircar sales campaign. Learning of Nancy's qualifications and her youth — she was now twenty-three—Bruno suggested that Nancy be made a member of the company's board of directors.

Gwinn, though sold on her aviation qualifications, wasn't sure this was a good idea. Nancy didn't fit the 1930's image of a corporate board member. Wrong sex. Too young. Too pretty. But that was exactly what Harry Bruno wanted. In his opinion, those assets and qualities equaled sex appeal.

"Socially she is everything that we would want," he wrote to Gwinn. "On top of it all, this young lady has an exceptionally good head and lends herself to the type of dignified publicity we have in mind for the Aircar. Properly presented to the public, she will be an asset."

Bruno wrote to Nancy asking for more details on her aviation career. She wrote back:

> I think the only claim I have to fame is that I probably have an awful lot of time on tricycle landing gear ships; I mean comparatively lots, as there aren't yet many pilots of either sex who have flown them. I think I have well over a hundred hours on the Hammond and the Gwinn.

Instead of sitting on the corporate board, Nancy was hired as assistant sales manager to sell the Aircar. She was paired with Hawks who had returned from Hollywood. He was named vice president in charge of sales of the Aircar.

Nancy made her final flight in the Aircar in June 1938 and returned to her work at Inter City. She had done what Joe Gwinn had asked her to do and she was ready to move on. She didn't fly the Aircar again and that was fate working in her favor.

On August 23, 1938, Hawks and a prospective customer climbed in the Aircar for a demonstration ride as a small crowd watched. They took off, cleared a fence, tilted sideways, flew between two tall trees, and passed over a hill out of sight. Moments later, the crowd heard a crash and saw flames rising over the hill. The group raced toward the flames and pulled Hawks and his passenger from beneath a burning wing. Both had been fatally injured.

Nancy moved on. This was not the last time she would face the death of someone with whom she worked.

Nancy Love with Frank Hawks in 1938 with the Gwinn Aircar. Love and Hawks worked to promote and sell the Aircar as a replacement for the family car. *Courtesy: The Love family collection.*

Chapter Four

WAR!

NANCY'S LIFE, AND THE LIVES OF ALL AMERICANS, changed when Germany invaded Poland on September 1, 1939. World War II had begun.

Aviation had grown from its barnstorming adolescence in the 1920s to a robust young adulthood by the late 1930s as commercial aviation caught on. In 1932, the press had dubbed Nancy Love "The Flying Freshman." Now, the young woman who hung around the local airport on weekends while a student at Vassar, was growing up.

At Inter City Aviation, Nancy and Bob Love sold popular aircraft such as the Beechcraft Staggerwing. Beechcraft's general sales manager William A. "Pappy" Ong, an admirer of Nancy and Bob Love, tried to recruit Nancy to fly one in the 1936 Bendix Race. Nancy received this telegram from Ong:

> Suggest you contact Louise Thaden by telegraph—she will be at factory tomorrow—and ask to go as copilot in Bendix Race. I think you would be of great assistance and it would be fine experience for you.

Fate was tempting Nancy, but this was not to be her turn for the brass ring. Louise, who was after Amelia Earhart the best-known woman flyer in the country, had already spoken to Blanche Noyes about going along as copilot. Nancy lost the opportunity of a lifetime—to fly copilot on the first woman-pilot team to win the prestigious Bendix.

When Louise and Blanche flew their Staggerwing to victory, they bested all the male pilots entered in the 2,500-mile race from New York to Los Angeles.

Once again Ong surprised Nancy by entering her in the Amelia Earhart Trophy Race. She had never raced before and yet managed to come in fifth. Two weeks later, she flew in the Women's Air Race, part of the Michigan Air Races in Detroit. She may have been the most surprised person there when she came in second.

That was the end of Nancy's brief air racing career. She disliked the haste and confusion.

By September 1939, Nancy had made quite a name for herself through her work with the Airmarking program, the Hammond Y, and the Gwinn Aircar. She was ready to move forward again.

✢ ✢ ✢

With the war on in Europe, Betty Gillies, president of the Ninety-Nines, the leading women pilots' organization, urged members to "upgrade your horsepower ratings, get your ratings. We may be needed if the USA enters the war."

Nancy and Betty were friends. Nancy, following her friend's suggestion, earned her instrument rating and also added a seaplane rating.

In the spring of 1940, the war was not going well for America's allies. The French were struggling to stop a German advance on their borders.

By 1940, Nancy had 825 flight hours. She knew other women pilots with similar experience. The United States was not in the war but faced an uncertain future and was building aircraft at an ever-increasing rate. There weren't enough licensed male pilots to fly those new planes. Pilots were in demand.

Nancy had an idea that could ease the shortage. Why not use women pilots? The Air Corps' Robert Olds was a friend of the

Loves. Nancy wrote to him, "Could you use qualified civilian women pilots to ferry airplanes for the U.S. Army?" [To ferry an aircraft means to fly that aircraft from one location to another where it is needed.]

Colonel Olds was interested and asked her for a list of women with a commercial [the highest] rating. She sent him those names as well as names of several women holding private licenses, who Nancy thought could handle the job.

"I've found forty-nine I can rate as excellent material. I think this list is up to handling pretty complicated stuff," she wrote to Olds.

Nancy's efforts were premature but not her instincts. Olds put the idea of civilian women ferrying aircraft on the back burner, but it wasn't dead. Nancy was on to something.

Inter City Aviation had a contract to ferry 31 aircraft to Canada. The planes were on their way to France. On June 2, 1940, Nancy, Bob and 29 male pilots left Boston for Halifax, Nova Scotia, Canada. At Houlton, Maine, on the border between the U.S. and Canada, the pilots climbed out of their aircraft. Since the United States was a neutral nation, it could not directly supply weapons to countries at war. The planes were pulled across the international boundary by trucks driven by Canadians.

Once the planes were across the border, the U.S. pilots climbed back in the cockpits and flew on to Halifax. Ten days later, Paris fell to the Germans and France surrendered. Even if the planes had been delivered, they would have been too late to help the French.

Bob Love, already in the Air Corps Reserves, was called to active duty on May 6, 1941. Olds asked Bob to join his new Ferrying Command operation.

On March 11, 1941, Congress passed the Lend-Lease Act. Now, the U. S. military could loan weapons to foreign countries, and the president could help "any country whose defense he deemed vital to the defense of the U.S."

Mr. and Mrs. Robert M. Love. *Courtesy: The Love family collection.*

U.S. pilots could now ferry aircraft across borders and the North Atlantic. Activity quickly increased at Houlton. Olds sent Major Bob Love to manage the Air Corps' personnel there.

In 1941, cosmetics-entrepreneur-turned-racing-pilot Jacqueline Cochran proposed an even bigger role for women pilots directly to President Franklin D. Roosevelt.

On Roosevelt's suggestion, Cochran met with Colonel Olds and H. H. "Hap" Arnold, the Commanding General of what soon would be known as the U.S. Army Air Forces. Cochran proposed using women pilots to replace male pilots wherever possible in order to free men for combat-related duty.

Cochran went to work on a formal proposal. In July 1941, she and members of her personal and business staff at Jacqueline

Cochran Cosmetics searched the Civil Aeronautics Administration (CAA) files for names of women pilots who might qualify. Her primary interest was to train a large number of women to take on a variety of aviation duties.

Olds invited Nancy Love to come to Washington so the two could meet. Maybe they could work together. Nancy and Jackie soon learned they were not on the same page. When compared, their ideas for how to use women pilots were quite different. It was the first of what would be many disagreements between the two.

General Olds summed up their differences on ferrying aircraft this way: "Miss Cochran did not believe that a woman could fly a plane more than a short distance, hence she was working out an elaborate system of relays. Mrs. Love thought this was quite unnecessary."

Nor did Olds and Cochran have the same vision for how to use the women pilots. He wanted a solution to the Army's immediate need for ferry pilots. She was laying the groundwork for a large women's pilot organization. Olds thought the scale of her proposal was far larger than was needed.

He told General Arnold he thought using women pilots was a good idea but pushed for Nancy Love's concept. "Let's set up a ninety-day service test for fifty women pilots with more than 500 hours flying time," he suggested. Then the Ferrying Command could employ the civilian women after determining that they were qualified.

General Arnold didn't think women could handle the Army's airplanes, even the small single-engine ones. He rejected both Cochran's and Olds's proposals.

Nancy Love went back to Boston. With Bob in Maine, she was now running Inter City Aviation by herself.

The British already were using women as ferry pilots. Trying to smooth ruffled feathers—after all Cochran was a friend of the Roosevelts—Arnold suggested the British contact Cochran to recruit American women pilots for service in England. They did, and by December she was recruiting American women to go to England and fly for the British Air Transport Auxiliary (ATA).

The morning of December 7, 1941, the island nation of Japan launched a surprise attack on the United States. Japanese fighter aircraft, flown off aircraft carriers, attacked the U.S. Naval Pacific fleet based at Pearl Harbor on the Hawaiian island of Oahu. The United States was now at war.

Olds was promoted to Brigadier General. As head of the Ferrying Command, he needed all the pilots he could lay his hands on, fast! New aircraft were coming off the factory assembly lines. Pilots to fly them were in short supply He resurrected Nancy Love's idea to use qualified women pilots. But he made a very big mistake. He let his plans slip to Cochran.

By now, Jackie Cochran was busily recruiting American women to go to England to fly for the ATA's women's squadrons. She asked Hap Arnold to stop Olds's plan. She wrote to Arnold:

> General Olds has informed me that he is planning on hiring women pilots for his Ferrying Command almost at once. His plan, as outlined to me, is not only bad in my opinion from the organizational standpoint, and contrary to what you told me yesterday but is in direct conflict, in fact, with the plans of a women's unit for England. In addition, it would wash me out of the supervision of the women flyers here rather than the contrary as we contemplated.

Arnold wrote to Olds, "You will make no plans or re-open negotiations for hiring women pilots until Miss Jacqueline Cochran has completed her present agreement with the British authorities and has returned to the United States."

Both Nancy Love's idea to use women pilots and Olds's intent to do so were put on hold.

Chapter Five

Enter: The WAFS

FOLLOWING THE JAPANESE ATTACK on Pearl Harbor, all airfields within 100 miles of the U.S. coastline were shut down for fear of enemy attack, Inter City Aviation among them.

Bob Love was relocated to Washington, D.C., and Nancy moved with him. In March 1942, with Bob Olds's recommendation, she went to work for a branch of the Ferrying Command located in nearby Baltimore, Maryland. Automobile gas was rationed, but aviation fuel was not, so Nancy flew to work in the family Fairchild 24.

Sure enough, Nancy had the aviation know-how Major Robert M. Baker, the officer-in-charge, needed, and he was quick to recognize it. Baker made her Operations Manager. Her job was to map ferry flights and routes, learn military procedures, and locate those badly needed pilots.

Again, Nancy proposed using qualified women fliers. Again, the idea was put on hold, but not for long.

When illness sidelined General Olds, General Harold L. George took Olds's place and changed the name to Air Transport Command (ATC). Colonel William H. Tunner became the commanding officer of the newly named Ferrying Division, the major arm of ATC.

Major Robert H. Baker and his Operations Manager Nancy
Love at the Ferrying Command Office, Baltimore, Spring 1942.
Courtesy: WASP Archive, Texas Woman's University, Denton.

Neither George nor Tunner was aware of the earlier discussions about hiring women pilots.

ATC's offices were located in the dingy basement of the old munitions building in Washington. Major Bob Love was now the ATC's Deputy Chief of Staff for Operations. At the water cooler one stormy spring morning, Bob mentioned that he hoped his wife had managed to land the family airplane safely in Baltimore and report for work.

General William H. Tunner, Commander, Ferrying Division, Air Transport Command, 1942-1944. *Courtesy: USAF.*

"Your wife flies!" Tunner said. "I'm combing the woods for pilots, and here's one right under my nose. Are there many more women like your wife?"

"Why don't you ask her?" Love replied.

Nancy Love made quite an impression on Colonel Tunner. Charming and attractive, she turned out to be savvy about aircraft and aviation, had 1,100 hours flight time, and she was full of workable ideas.

"Yes," she told him, "there are nearly a hundred proven, capable women pilots out there—probably more."

Tunner recognized ability when he saw it. Here was a woman to be reckoned with. They got down to business, and what an ally she turned out to be.

Colonel Robert H. Baker. *Courtesy: Robert Patterson, Baker's grandson.*

"Mrs. Love and I prepared a lengthy memorandum proposing a complete program for acquiring, training, and using women pilots."

Nancy went to work immediately drafting a plan to recruit women pilots, who would work as Civil Service employees, not as members of the military, at least for the present. Militarization was a future possibility, but Nancy and Tunner preferred to get the program off the ground first and worry about that later.

To qualify, a woman needed 500 hours, a commercial license, a 200-horsepower rating—and be between ages twenty-one and thirty-five. Suggested salary was $250 a month, fifty dollars less than civilian male ferry pilots received. This was because the women would be assigned to ferry light, less complicated aircraft.

Colonel Tunner lined up living quarters and dining privileges for the women pilots at New Castle Army Air Base (NCAAB) in Wilmington, Delaware. Major Baker, now a Colonel, had been named base commander. Male pilots and women ferry pilots assigned there would be part of the 2nd Ferrying Group.

Tunner chose NCAAB because it was close to Hagerstown, Maryland, home of the Fairchild Aviation Corporation that built the primary trainers he needed the women to ferry. [Primary trainers, known as PTs, were used in the first phase of military flight training.]

Together, Nancy and Lt. Joe Tracy, one of Baker's top-flight instructors, wrote the women pilots' training curriculum. Coming up with a uniform for her women pilots was her next task. Nancy was also appointed an unofficial member of the three-man board that would interview the women pilot applicants.

Still waiting for a final go-ahead from General Arnold, Colonel Baker, Colonel Tunner and Nancy continued their planning.

On September 5, Arnold directed them to begin recruiting women pilots. Nancy and Colonel Baker sent telegrams to eighty-three women pilots they thought might qualify.

The afternoon of September 10, 1942, General George accompanied Nancy Love to the office of the Secretary of War, who made the public announcement of her appointment as head of a new women's pilot group.

Nancy Love (right) sits in at the three-man review board, New Castle Army Air Base, 1942. Colonel Baker (center) and two of his staff officers are interviewing WAFS hopeful Helen Mary Clark. *Courtesy: Robert Patterson.*

Chapter Six

Cochran Comes Home

NANCY'S APPOINTMENT AS HEAD OF THE Women's Auxiliary Ferrying Squadron made news. The *New York Times* printed the story the following morning, accompanied by a photograph of Nancy Love and General George shaking hands.

Jacqueline Cochran arrived back in New York from England on September 10. The next morning, she took one look at the *Times* front page and left immediately for Washington, D.C., and a showdown with Hap Arnold. Hadn't he intended that job for her?

Brandishing a copy of the *New York Times,* she demanded to know what this story was all about. Arnold told her he "had given instructions to prepare and submit plans for the use of women pilots, but that he had not seen the plan."

A memo to General George from Arnold contradicts that statement. ATC historian Colonel Oliver LaFarge wrote, "General Arnold acted on General George's memorandum on September 5, which set forth the plan fully."

Cochran claimed that Arnold had promised her the leadership role in any women pilots' organization. She handed Arnold a memo that she had just prepared:

> The use of a few of our women pilots to ferry trainer planes is just one segment of a larger job to be done.

General Harold L. George congratulates Nancy Love, named Squadron Commander of the Women's Auxiliary Ferrying Squadron, September 10, 1942. *Courtesy: WASP Archive, Texas Woman's University, Denton.*

Failing to properly coordinate all the women pilot resources would be wasteful. You told me I would do the top job and this is the one I have been preparing to do during the past year.

Arnold called General George into his office. In Cochran's presence, Arnold told him that the project should be revised and that he should work it out with Cochran for she knew his views.

General George went to work and drafted this two-part memo to General Arnold.

- The ATC would employ fifty experienced women ferry pilots. No training of additional women pilots was planned. Nor did the ATC have training facilities.
- The Flying Training Command in Texas was actively training male pilots. The program was easily adaptable to train women. After the women pilots graduated, they would be assigned to the ATC for ferrying duty.

Arnold announced publicly that Cochran would form and lead a second women's program, the Women's Flying Training Detachment (WFTD), to train more women pilots to ferry airplanes for the ATC.

On September 15, Cochran met with representatives of the ATC, Air Staff, and the Civil Aeronautics Association (CAA) to develop a plan based on General George's memo.

Colonel Tunner, not realizing how big a storm was brewing, sent Captain James I. Teague as ATC's representative to that meeting. Teague, smart and intuitive but only a lowly captain, was flanked by a determined Jacqueline Cochran and by fellow officers who held the rank of colonel or higher. They hammered out the plan for training and using women pilots.

Teague sensed that Cochran had it in for the ATC and the Ferrying Division. She wanted to be director of *all* the women pilots flying for the Army and have them organized into a separate women's corps, answerable to her. He thought she was looking for ways to undo what had been done.

"I have a definite feeling of suspicion in regard to the actions of Miss Jacqueline Cochran," Teague told Turner. "This is principally a hunch, but I am convinced that we should probably do something about it, and convey to General Arnold our attitude toward her. She considers herself the only person who could efficiently be in charge of the Women Ferry Pilots."

Jacqueline Cochran in her WASP uniform. *Courtesy: Coachella Valley History Museum, Indio, California.*

Teague told Tunner that he was asked to agree to have "one of our male flight officers or transition officers at Wilmington give the flight check, and not to let Mrs. Love give a flight check on a woman who had already been flight checked by Miss Cochran.

"Miss Cochran, as far as the public is concerned, is coming to us and bringing us women who have been trained, and we should be appreciative. I, on the other hand, fear the Greeks bearing gifts." [An allusion to the Roman poet Virgil's *Aeneid*.]

Colonel Tunner, in turn, reported to General George and added his personal take.

> [Graduates] will be employed at Headquarters, 2nd Ferrying Group, Ferrying Division, ATC . . . only if they meet the basic requirements for the position of women civilian pilots (including physical examination and flight test) and not because they have graduated from the course outlined above.

Tunner believed he had the right to turn down flight school graduates if he felt they didn't meet Ferrying Division standards. General George, fearing General Arnold's wrath, continually cautioned Tunner to go easy in turning down graduates.

It was decided that Nancy Love would continue to lead the existing squadron of between 25 and 50 women. Cochran had the go-ahead to put in motion a facility to train more women pilots to fly for the Ferrying Division.

If only Cochran had been satisfied.

Arnold had a war to fight. He took the easy way out. He let Cochran make it seem the ATC was wrong to start the WAFS program and to appoint Nancy even though he knew that George and Tunner had worked throughout the summer of 1942 to form a woman's ferrying squadron.

Cochran blamed the ATC, General George, C.R. Smith, the Ferrying Division, Colonel Tunner, Nancy Love, and Bob Love for what she perceived as an attempt to wrest from her the leadership of the women pilots that she felt was hers by right.

Hap Arnold had intentionally surrounded himself with bright young men. His instructions to them: "Think of the problems confronting us. Think of the solutions to those problems. Bring in new ideas. Don't get mixed up with the routine operations of this office. Think of the future of the Air Force!"

"I turned people loose and forgot about them," he wrote after the war.

The Air Transport Command, he said, was a case in point. "Once it had established its bases around the world, and General George and Gen. C. R. Smith were operating it, I was able to forget about it."

Arnold had handpicked Smith to work with George. Yet, in Smith, Cochran found her scapegoat. That C. R. Smith was one of Nancy Love's most powerful and staunch supporters probably contributed to Cochran's animosity.

The ATC was not interested in large numbers of women pilots, only in securing pilots of either sex who met its high standards.

"What created the problem was that Cochran was determined that the ATC would accept all the women flyers that graduated from the Training Command's school," ATC historian Col. Oliver LaFarge wrote after the war.

Colonel Tunner wanted to employ only those who met ATC standards.

Captain Teague warned Tunner, "Miss Cochran will take inch by inch and try to move in on us." He proved to be correct.

"Cochran made it quite clear that she . . . would do everything possible to take control of the WAFS away from the ATC," WASP historian Deborah Douglas wrote.

> The two women's pilots programs were highly visible pawns in this struggle—Cochran had recognized this fact in her first encounter with Robert Olds. [Nancy] Love was not ignorant of the dynamics involved, but she did not believe it was appropriate or useful to exploit the situation. Cochran had no qualms about pressing her views.

On September 1, 1942, the Army had no women's flying programs. By September 15, it had two.

Chapter Seven

A Study in Contrasts

AT WILMINGTON, NANCY LOVE began interviewing candidates for the WAFS. Jackie Cochran soon would be on her way to Texas to set up the women's flight training facility and recruit the first WFTD trainees.

A news story in the September 25 issue of the *Washington Daily News* caught Colonel Tunner's attention. The article included this quote from Cochran,

> Yes, I've been called back by General Arnold to be head of a women's air corps in this country. Our goal is 1,500. I've had such success with my girls in England that I know this will work.

Colonel Tunner did not like Cochran's methods. She threw her weight around. She gave exaggerated statements to the press, like the one above, and no one fact-checked them. She tried to strong arm Captain Teague, who Tunner had sent to the meeting between Cochran and Ferrying Division officers to work out the details of bringing the WFTC graduates into the Ferrying Division. The generals and colonels outranked Teague at the meeting. But he was unfalteringly Tunner's man.

Tunner feared an influx of 1,500 newly trained women pilots would lower the Division's standards. He asked a friend in London to do some checking on Cochran's program there.

He learned that the American women pilots serving with the Air Transport Auxiliary were doing just fine. However, the British military resented Cochran's flamboyant behavior and embellishment of her importance. Cochran had no actual role in the women's training in England. Her job was voluntary and unpaid. She simply had organized and brought the women to the ATA to serve.

Tunner wanted more women pilots. If they could meet his standards, he welcomed them. Trying to keep Tunner from alienating General Arnold on the matter of Cochran's women pilots, General George cautioned Tunner to step carefully in order not to alienate General Arnold, who supported Cochran's idea.

"Cochran's success in playing hardball politics came at a stiff cost," historian Douglas wrote. "She had alienated the people and organizations that should have been her most important allies: Love, the ATC, and Col. Oveta Culp Hobby, the commandant of the Women's Army Corps (WAC). Unlike Cochran, Love recognized the need for flexibility and compromise."

Love believed that experienced women pilots could offer modest assistance to the war effort. Love also knew that the WAFS could not begin ferrying airplanes as long as the top brass squabbled over the details. In her mind it was far better to get on with the flying, then work out the details. For Cochran, it was of primary importance that the women pilots serve under her command.

The fight for the leadership of the Army's women pilots would not go away.

✯ ✯ ✯

The world was changing. The war was bringing about a social upheaval that affected society as a whole and in the long run, the role of women would be one of the most changed.

General George had observed Nancy Love throughout the summer of 1942 and the September leadership skirmishes. He was impressed with her good judgment and calm, discrete manner she brought to the job.

Nancy was not timid. She *was* ambitious and confident in her ability to recruit women pilots to fly any and all aircraft the Army would let them fly. And Nancy was determined to fly every aircraft she could get her hands on. She expected to fly on-the-job and continue to lead by example.

"On the surface, Nancy played the game," said Barbara (BJ) Erickson, who Nancy appointed in January 1943 to lead the women's squadron with the 6th Ferrying Group in Long Beach, California. "She was practical, sensible, reserved. But underneath was this bubbling cauldron, a desire to accomplish things. And she was very strong-willed."

Nancy Love may not have been competitive by nature, but she had put a lot of time, thought, effort, and heart into the WAFS. She was not going to walk away from a solution she was certain would help win the war.

She also wanted to fly the Army's airplanes — bigger, faster, all of them! As was typical of American men *and women* in WWII, she wanted to serve her country, and preferably from the cockpit of an Army airplane, not by flying a desk.

Command was not her goal. Proving to the men that women could fly military airplanes was her goal. But command is what she got. As the leader of the Women's Auxiliary Ferrying Squadron, she proved to be very good at the job.

Nancy sends the first WAFS candidate, Betty Gillies, off on a PT-19 check flight, September 10, 1942. *Courtesy: The Love family collection.*

Chapter Eight

The Originals Gather

BETTY GILLIES, AGE THIRTY-FIVE, flew from Syosset, Long Island, to Wilmington the day after she received Nancy's telegram inviting her to join the squadron. She was the first to arrive.

"You don't have to stay for long," Nancy told her good friend. "Just the first ninety days until we get started." For Betty, ninety days turned into twenty-eight months. In her diary Betty noted that she was the first woman to sign up for the required ninety-day commitment. She was instructed to report for duty at 8 a.m. on September 21.

By the time Betty returned on the 21st, seven others had passed their flight tests, joined her on the roster, and moved into the newly opened Bachelor Officers Quarters (BOQ #14): Cornelia Fort, Aline "Pat" Rhonie, Helen Mary Clark, Catherine Slocum, Adela "Del" Scharr, Esther Nelson, and Teresa James.

BOQ 14 had housed men. Getting it ready for women took some modifications. Nancy ordered Venetian blinds for the windows and had wood planks installed over the ditch that ran in front of the entrance.

In late September, the younger women began to arrive. The first eight, except for twenty-three-year-old Cornelia Fort, were married and ranged in age from late twenties to thirty-five-years old. The younger twenty-somethings that came to Wilmington

Nancy Love and Colonel Baker review the first eight WAFS: Betty Gillies, Esther Nelson, Cornelia Fort, Teresa James, Catherine Slocum, Del Scharr, Helen Mary Clark (hidden behind Love) and Aline Rhonie. *Courtesy: Robert Patterson.*

were unmarried, and many were graduates of the pre-war Civilian Pilot Training Program that taught college-age men and some women to fly. All had been employed teaching Army and Navy cadets, men younger than themselves, how to fly in preparation for wartime military aviation.

On October 6, Betty Gillies was named Nancy's executive officer. That meant she was second in command and in charge when Nancy was off base.

October 19 was graduation day for the first nine WAFS. Then, Catherine Slocum, the mother of four, resigned. Plans for the care of her children had gone awry, and she was needed at home.

Nancy selected the WAFS uniform: a tailored, gray-green wool gabardine jacket with squared shoulders, brass buttons, straight set-in

Nancy Love in the WAFS dress uniform. *Courtesy: The Love family collection.*

sleeves, and a matching detached belt. The uniform included a gored skirt for street wear and slacks for flying. Shirts and ties were of tan broadcloth. Brown leather low-heeled pumps, a brown leather shoulder bag, an overcoat, and gloves completed the outfit.

The women paid for their own uniforms and were required to wear them while on ferrying duty or on base. The WAFS wore the civilian pilot wings of the Air Transport Command pinned over the jacket left breast pocket. They were issued khaki flight coveralls (made to fit men, therefore far too large for most of the women), a parachute, goggles, a white silk AAF flying scarf, and leather flying jackets with the distinctive ATC patch.

WAFS in coveralls stand ready to ferry the PT-19s behind them. Helen Mary Clark, Aline "Pat" Rhonie, Catherine Slocum, and Cornelia Fort. *Courtesy: Robert Patterson.*

The WAFS' first ferrying assignment was October 22-23, 1942.

Betty Gillies led a flight of six small single-engine liaison planes called L-4Bs. These were known in civilian life as Piper Cubs.

Fort, Clark, Rhonie, Scharr, and James made up her team. The WAFS picked up the planes from the Piper factory in Lock Haven, Pennsylvania, and flew them to Mitchel Field on Long Island.

Teresa James recalled that every man on the field lined up to watch, expecting them all to crash. The women all made quite good landings, Teresa said, adding that the men seemed surprised and rather disappointed.

When Betty reported to the officer-in-charge, he yelled at her that he "needed them two months ago!"

"That's not my problem," she said sweetly. "I'm merely following my orders. You may speak to my commanding officer, Col. Robert Baker at New Castle Army Air Base, or call Colonel Tunner himself at Ferrying Division headquarters." She gave the man a big smile.

November 20, eleven WAFS left to deliver the first of many PT-19 primary trainer aircraft. They flew eleven Fairchild open-cockpit, single-engine, 175-horsepower trainers to Army flight training bases located mostly in the Southern states where the weather was better. The PT-19 would be used to train inexperienced male pilots to fly.

The arrival of November meant a change for the worse in weather. Frequently, the women were forced to land and wait out bad weather en route and had to RON (remain overnight) wherever they stopped. If the weather was particularly bad, it took them several days to get the planes to their destinations.

Dorothy Scott, WAFS number twenty-five, arrived in Wilmington on November 21.

"The Originals," as the first WAFS are known today, in the order they joined, were, Nancy Love, Betty Gillies, Cornelia Fort, Aline "Pat" Rhonie, Helen Mary Clark, Adela "Del" Scharr, Esther Nelson, Teresa James, Barbara Poole, Helen Richards, Barbara Towne, Gertrude Meserve, Florene Miller, Barbara Jane "BJ" Erickson, Delphine Bohn, Barbara "Donnie" Donahue, Evelyn Sharp, Phyllis Burchfield, Esther Manning, Nancy Batson, Katherine "Kay" Rawls Thompson, Dorothy Fulton, Opal "Betsy" Ferguson, Bernice Batten, and Dorothy Scott.

Three more would join. On January 3, 1943, Helen McGilvery and Sis Bernheim passed their flight tests. Lenore McElroy became the final member of the original WAFS on January 23.

In the meantime, Pat Rhonie left following a conflict with Colonel Baker over unauthorized leave.

Nancy was the squadron's disciplinarian, but she needed someone on-site to organize and run BOQ 14. She and Colonel Baker hired Mrs. Anderson (Andy) to serve as housemother.

"We weren't teenagers," Gertrude Meserve said. "But I guess it just sounded better to our parents if we had a housemother, even though several of the women were married and a couple had children."

Once they had uniforms and a sufficient number of WAFS to practice marching, Colonel Baker ordered them to march in the Saturday morning review with the male troops stationed at NCAAB. In the military, this is called close order drill.

One Friday night, the whole group decided to go dancing at Wilmington's posh DuPont Hotel. Nancy Batson, who had picked up a bad cold, joined them anyway and danced away the night. Of course, she could hardly drag herself out of bed the next morning.

"I got my robe on and staggered down the hall to Nancy Love's room," Nancy recalled. "She was already dressed for the review. I said, 'Miz Love, I just don't think I can march this morning, I've got this *awful* cold and feel just lousy.'

"Nancy, didn't I see you out dancing at the DuPont Hotel last night?"

"I hung my head and studied my feet for a minute, then said, 'Yes, ma'am.'

"Well then, Nancy, I think you can manage to march this morning."

"We were obliged to learn close order drill," Nancy Love wrote. "As Commander, I had to lead the formation and give the commands, which, because I was very self-conscious, was not one of my strong points. In fact, I so hated having to roar out orders that I occasionally drew a blank on what command to give next."

One morning the squadron was marching down the paved runway toward a steep embankment at the end.

"Panic struck me as we approached the precipice," Nancy wrote, "and I found myself incapable of giving the command, 'To the rear—march!'

"So off went twenty-four girls, still in close formation and roaring with laughter. Straight down the embankment they went and into the field below, leaving me standing at the top, still speechless."

Once the press learned that women were being hired to fly airplanes for the Army, the base was deluged with reporters and photographers and requests for interviews. The WAFS realized that they were looked on as if they were the story of the century. The women did not welcome the spotlight.

"No one had anticipated the widespread publicity," Delphine Bohn wrote. "The military was deeply affronted that this strange, multifaceted publicity could afflict them so. Everyone wished to examine each of us minutely. It was purely terrorizing."

Many of the stories written about the women pilots were blatantly incorrect, grossly exaggerated, or just plain fabricated. One reporter dreamed up a fake story of the women ferrying aircraft at night and through a storm. The Ferrying Division did not ferry aircraft at night.

Following several requests from magazines for ghostwritten accounts of WAFS on duty, Colonel Tunner put a ban on sensationalized publicity. "Stories of this type are not considered to be for the best interests of the Ferrying Division and will tend to overglamorize the members of the WAFS."

One story about Mrs. Love was true, but it had nothing to do with what Nancy was doing for her country as the newly appointed head of the WAFS. Nancy made the list of "Best Legs Among Women in Public Life in America 1942." She was in the company of movie star Dorothy Lamour and radio star Gracie Allen of "The Burns and Allen Show."

The press begged her to "give us a smile, a big one. Show your teeth." Worse, she was subjected to requests for "cheesecake shots," showing lots of leg or a bare shoulder.

The Army tried to protect the women from the spotlight, but they were under both the bright glare of publicity and the microscope of public opinion. To their credit, not a word of scandal was ever connected with any of the original WAFS during the time they served Uncle Sam.

Once they began ferrying, eight to ten girls headed out on a trip, leaving eight to ten behind—some still in orientation training. The women arrived at different times during the fall and tended to make friendships in twos and threes—those who arrived together, those who were the same age or from the same area, those who had similar outside interests.

Most close friendships developed on ferrying trips. Frequently, two or more WAFS were grounded in the same place by bad weather along their delivery routes. When stuck on some airfield with nothing to do but wait out the weather, the women began to share their life stories with each other.

The WAFS flew in groups because they were ferrying slower airplanes that needed frequent refueling. Often, several were destined for the same base. But already the lonely nature of the job had been revealed to them, something that would become second nature when they began ferrying coast to coast alone.

Chapter Nine

Growing Pains

WHILE NANCY LOVE WAS BUILDING her squadron, Jacqueline Cochran was in Fort Worth working with the Army's Flying Training Command (FTC) to organize and implement a flight-training program for women pilots.

General Arnold wanted 500 women pilots qualified to fly small Army aircraft by the end of 1943. The Training Command would provide the instruction. Upon graduation, the women would be sent to fly for the Ferrying Division, an arm of the Air Transport Command (ATC).

The ATC asked that the women have a minimum of 300 hours flying time — the same as male candidates — to qualify for acceptance into the program. ATC lost that battle. The compromise was 200. Cochran soon lowered that requirement to 75 hours. By April 1943, the women needed only 35 hours — the number required for a private pilot's license.

Nancy was not involved in the battle between Cochran and the ATC. She concentrated on her growing squadron and getting her women pilots ready for their first ferrying trips.

On November 16, Cochran's first class of twenty-nine trainees began learning to fly "the Army way" at Houston Municipal Airport. A second class of fifty-one women reported December 13.

The Great Falls Six in front of the six PT-17 Stearmans they ferried: Katherine Rawls Thompson, Phyllis Burchfield, Nancy Batson, Delphine Bohn, Florene Miller, Teresa James. *Courtesy: Author's Personal Collection, gift of Teresa James.*

The Ferrying Division began planning to incorporate these women into the WAFS.

Nancy sent six WAFS by train to Great Falls, Montana. The Canadian RAF was returning thirty-three bi-wing Stearman PT-17 trainers, on loan from the Ferrying Division. The open-cockpit trainers were useless during the cold Canadian winter. The aircraft needed to be relocated in a warmer climate.

The six women joined twenty-seven male ferry pilots to move the thirty-three trainers to Jackson, Tennessee. Nancy named Teresa James flight leader.

At the same time, Colonel Tunner sent Nancy and several Ferrying Division officers to visit the other six ATC ferrying bases to determine if they would accept a women's squadron and, if so, to recommend the arrangements that would be needed to house and feed those women.

Nancy and the officers arrived in Great Falls on December 11, the day before her women pilots departed in their six Stearmans for Jackson. Nancy's traveling party was there to talk to the command of the 7th Ferrying Group about housing a WAFS squadron.

That night, Nancy met with her six women pilots and told them the WAFS were being split up. A few of them would be assigned to each of the bases that accepted women. Several were to remain in Wilmington as part of the 2nd Ferrying Group. The first graduates from Houston would arrive in the spring to augment the numbers of each of the squadrons.

Teresa, never shy, spoke up immediately. "If some of us are going to Long Beach, I want to be one of them." Teresa's husband was stationed in the Long Beach area.

Nancy and the male officers left Great Falls on December 13. They flew to Long Beach, California, home of the 6th Ferrying Group and the ATC's largest base. Knowing that the WAFS assigned there would be ferrying the larger basic trainer (BT) aircraft, Nancy checked out in the single-engine, 450-horsepower BT-13 built at the nearby Vultee factory.

On the group's flight from Phoenix to Dallas, she flew as pilot-in-command of the Vultee twin-engine C-36. In Dallas, she met with officials from the 5th Ferrying Group at Love Field. [No connection to Bob Love or his family.]

Her mission not over, Nancy next went to Memphis to talk to the 4th Ferrying Group. On December 20, she was in Romulus, Michigan, at the Wayne County Airport where she conferred with the command of the 3rd Ferrying Group.

Back in Washington, Nancy and the Ferrying Division officials compiled what they had learned. Women's ferrying squadrons

WAFS Betsy Ferguson, Florene Miller, and Helen Richards, all stationed at Dallas Love Field. *Courtesy: Author's Personal Collection.*

would be formed at Love Field in Dallas, at Romulus, and at Long Beach, in that order.

Florene Miller would lead the Love Field contingent. Going to Texas with her were Helen Richards, Dorothy Scott, and Betsy Ferguson. Nancy, too, was going to Dallas, but she put Florene in charge. Nancy had bigger things in mind and would be stationed there only briefly.

First, she planned to fly to Romulus and Long Beach to help establish those new squadrons. After that, she would travel between squadrons periodically to check on her pilots.

Nancy's strategy was to check out on every available aircraft to pave the way for the WAFS to fly everything in the Army's aviation

WAFS Katherine Rawls Thompson, Lenore McElroy, Barbara Poole, Barbara Donahue, Del Scharr, were stationed at Romulus. *Courtesy: International Women's Air and Space Museum (IWASM).*

arsenal. Already, she was pressuring Flight Operations for increased transition for the women. [*Transition* means to move up in size, classification, and power of aircraft.]

Del Scharr would command the Romulus group consisting of Barbara Donahue, Barbara Poole, Katherine Thompson, and Phyllis Burchfield.

Leader of the Long Beach pilots was Barbara Jane (BJ) Erickson and stationed with her were Cornelia Fort, Evelyn Sharp, Barbara Towne, and Bernice Batten. The rest remained in Wilmington with Betty Gillies in command.

Four of the WAFS sent to Long Beach: Evelyn Sharp, Nancy Love, Barbara Towne, and BJ Erickson boarding a C-47. *Courtesy: The Love family collection.*

The women would be scattered from coast to coast. Life in the WAFS would never be the same.

As 1942 ended, twenty-four WAFS were ferrying liaison airplanes and primary trainers. Nancy, herself, did not begin ferrying until January 1943, and even then her activities were limited because of her command responsibilities.

When the six who ferried the Stearmans to Tennessee returned to Wilmington on New Year's Day, Pat Rhonie was already gone. The women assigned to Dallas left within a couple of days. Nancy flew to Dallas New Year's Day.

Lenore McElroy, second-in-command, WAFS Romulus. *Courtesy: WASP Archive, Texas Woman's University, Denton.*

The first thing she did there was check out on an AT-6, the 600-horsepower, single-engine advanced trainer. Eventually, the Dallas women would fly the AT-6, built at nearby North American Aviation. Nancy flew the AT-6 to Romulus on January 13 to help Del Scharr establish her new squadron. The Michigan weather closed in, and Nancy was grounded there for several days. When the low cloud ceiling finally lifted, she flight-tested Lenore McElroy, a 35-year-old flight instructor with 3,500 hours.

The wife of a Romulus ferry pilot and mother of three teenagers, Lenore was accepted into the Romulus women's squadron on January 23, 1943, becoming the final member of the Original WAFS.

On January 25, General Arnold's office sent a message to Colonel Tunner stating that, from that date, the Ferrying Division would employ only those women who had graduated from the Women's Flying Training School in Texas.

"This was a big blow to the Command," says Betty Gillies. "There were still many eligible women pilots and the first graduates from WFTD would not be available until May, almost four months away. The pilot shortage continued to be a matter of great concern."

In February, Nancy asked for a transfer from Dallas to Long Beach, California, where her third new squadron would be located. Though she was going there to help organize the new squadron, advancement into higher-powered aircraft was very much on her mind. Many of the airplanes flown by the Army Air Forces in World War II were built in the greater Los Angeles area known as the LA Basin. Nancy planned to fly them all.

"She wanted to see if her stature and strength, and therefore most of her girls' stature and strength, would be a limiting factor," Barbara Erickson London pointed out. "Were there complications? She was looking not just at her limitations, but others' as well."

Nancy had Colonel Tunner's OK to fly any airplane she thought she could handle. Her sights were set on the sleek P-51, the fastest of the single-engine pursuit aircraft. Pursuits were high performance fighter aircraft with room for only one pilot. One's first flight in a pursuit was a solo—no instructor on board.

Nancy familiarized herself with the technical specifications of the P-51. Late in February she met Major Samuel C. Dunlap, III, at the end of an isolated runway where her first pursuit was parked. Dunlap was an old friend of both the Loves, and he was the Operations Officer for the 6th Ferrying Group at Long Beach.

She climbed in. Sam gave her a cockpit check and waved her off. Nancy could not see over the massive engine in front of her. She "S-ed" or zigzagged, down the taxiway in order to see if there was anything blocking her way as she taxied the plane.

The moment of truth for any fledgling pursuit pilot comes when she sits, alone, at the end of the runway. The engine roars. She stands on the brakes to harness all that pent-up power and keep the aircraft grounded a few more seconds.

Nancy released the brakes and pushed the throttle forward to the firewall, using the aircraft's full power. The P-51 surged forward. The tail lifted. Now she could see straight down the runway. The wind caught under the wings, lifted the aircraft, and carried it swiftly up into the California sky.

The Mustang, she discovered, flew like any other airplane, only faster. The response to the stick and rudders was immediate and sweet. For an hour, she practiced maneuvers aloft. Then she began her descent, bleeding off altitude and, finally, set up for her first landing. Moments later she was down and rolling along the runway.

When asked later about her historic flight, Nancy said, simply, that she felt "the same lonely but wonderful feeling you get on your first solo."

Major Dunlap signed off in her logbook. "Qualified at Long Beach, Calif."

The date was February 27, 1943. A woman had just flown one of the fastest airplanes ever built.

"Boy what news your call brought! You've just about reached the top!" Bob wrote to her that very same night, after learning from her via telephone that she had flown the P-51. But he also wrote, "I'm so afraid you will be so famous and involved with things that you won't care for the things that we have longed for before."

Chapter Ten

The WAFS Lose One

ORIGINAL WAFS CORNELIA FORT died March 21, 1943, in a mid-air collision near Merkel, Texas. Cornelia had been with Nancy Love from the beginning, arriving in Wilmington one day after Betty Gillies.

The official Army accident report read:
On March 21 at approximately 15:30 CWT (Central War Time) seven ships were proceeding East in formation, in the vicinity of Merkel, Texas. Of these seven ships, one BT-13A flown by Civilian Pilot Cornelia Fort and [a] BT-13A flown by F/O Frank E. Stamme, Jr., were involved in a mid-air collision. [F/O stands for flight officer.]

Cornelia and six male pilots were ferrying basic trainers to Dallas. Flying over sparsely inhabited West Texas, they took part in some formation flying. Though the WAFS' instructions were to stay 500 feet away from any other airplane, it appears Cornelia chose to ignore the order.

The landing gear of the other BT struck the wing of Cornelia's plane, causing the end of that wing to break off. Cornelia's plane rolled over into a dive from which she never recovered.

Cornelia Fort, the third pilot to join the WAFS. *Courtesy: WASP Archive, Texas Woman's University, Denton.*

Once before, Cornelia had looked death in the face while flying an airplane. While a flight instructor at Honolulu's John Rodgers Airport, she was flying with a student on the morning of

December 7, 1941. A Japanese Zero shot at them, but she managed to land safely in a hail of bullets.

Word of her death spread quickly through the WAFS' ranks. Cornelia was well liked. Her fellow WAFS knew her to be a solid flyer.

Cornelia's death deeply affected Nancy. Intellectually the WAFS leader knew that it had been Cornelia's choice—and that of all her women pilots—to join the squadron. But suddenly Nancy was in an unfamiliar role, that of a wartime commander who had just lost a trusted lieutenant.

Nancy and BJ Erickson, Cornelia's squadron commander, attended the funeral in Nashville. Nancy, uncomfortable with speaking in public, declined an invitation to speak. Instead, she wrote a letter to Cornelia's mother.

> My feeling about the loss of Cornelia is hard to put into words—I can only say that I miss her terribly, and loved her. She was a rare person. If there can be any comforting thought it is that she died as she wanted to—in an Army airplane, and in the service of her country.

The WAFS was Nancy's creation. She handpicked her pilots. Now one was gone.

"Nancy lived in an ordered world," BJ Erickson London said of the WAFS leader many years later. "Everything she did was well thought out and concise. Those who worked with her assumed the same position. She did not emote. She handled herself and the situation calmly."

In March 1943, the women ferry pilots were on the threshold of flying the Army's newest, hottest, airplanes. Caution was Nancy's rule. By long-standing habit, she followed her checklists to the letter, leaving nothing to chance. She took every precaution before leaving the ground. She hoped that her girls did the same. Once in the air, she did her job. She flew the airplane.

Chapter Eleven

Transport and Transition

CORNELIA WAS EXONERATED OF ANY BLAME for the accident that took her life, but the incident alarmed some of the men in the Ferry Command. Almost immediately, new restrictions came from the 3rd Ferrying Group in Romulus:

1) Women pilots would be allowed to fly only light trainer aircraft. (This meant women could not transition into basic or advanced trainers or twin-engine aircraft.)
2) Women would not be given assignments as copilots on bomber ferrying missions.
3) Women would not be allowed to transition on any high-powered single-engine or twin-engine aircraft.
4) In order to "protect" their morals, women would make their deliveries on alternate days from the male pilots. AND, they were to be—if at all possible—sent in opposite directions.

"Mrs. Love objected to this directive," a Ferrying Division representative pointed out.

Her objection to those restrictions was mild compared to her reaction to the next restrictions sent straight from ATC headquarters to group commanders.

1) No woman was to be assigned to flying duty when pregnant.
2) Women were not to fly one day before, through two days after, their menstrual period.

Mrs. Love was livid! The menstrual period restriction meant a wasteful eight or nine days of non-flying time per month per WAFS. The women pilots couldn't believe it.

Male staff had become concerned about physiological problems of women in relation to flying activities. By then one of the original WAFS, Esther Manning [married name Rathfelder] was pregnant. However, Betty Gillies, Esther's mature and perceptive squadron leader at Wilmington, had solved the problem.

Betty let Esther fly until she couldn't get the stick back in the cramped confines of the PT-19s. [Pulling the control stick back into one's stomach is one of the maneuvers necessary to land an aircraft.] Then Betty grounded Esther and put her to work as Operations Officer, thus allowing Betty, herself, and her executive officer Helen Mary Clark to get out of the office and fly more.

Nancy went over the heads of both Group and Ferrying Division Commanders and appealed the menstrual period ban, as well as the prohibition on transition, to her friend Gen. C. R. Smith, Chief of Staff of the ATC. She risked Colonel Tunner's ire by ignoring the chain of command and was, in fact, not in his good graces for some time after that.

General Smith, in a letter dated April 17, 1943, addressed Nancy Love's concern about the transition restrictions. The Ferrying Division, he said, had imposed certain flight limitations on women pilots *without* consideration of individual professional qualifications. He wrote, "It is the desire of this Command that all pilots, regardless of sex, be privileged to advance to the extent of their ability in keeping with the progress of aircraft development."

This was THE breakthrough the women pilots needed!

Colonel Tunner further clarified ATC's position in an April 26 memo to the commanding officers of all Ferrying Groups.

"Those at the bottom of the ladder will deliver the simplest forms of aircraft. Gradually . . . they will work their way from short hops in trainers on clear days to delivering the largest aircraft all over the world."

He reminded them this worked for male and female ferry pilots. If the women ferried only aircraft at the bottom of the transition ladder, men who needed to begin at that level would be denied that necessary training. Keeping the women permanently on the lowest level would create a bottleneck.

Tunner opened transition to the women pilots. Like the men, they could advance according to their ability and gain the experience needed to qualify to ferry any airplane in the Ferrying Division's inventory.

At a staff meeting on April 28, Tunner explained his new classification system.

- Class I—qualified to fly low-powered single-engine airplanes.
- Class II—qualified to fly twin-engine trainers and utility planes.
- Class III—qualified to fly twin-engine cargo/medium-transport planes.
- Class III-P—qualified to fly single engine, high-performance pursuits or fighters.
- Class IV—qualified to fly twin-engine planes in advanced categories, such as attack planes, medium bombers and heavier transports.
- Class IV-P—qualified to fly the twin-engine pursuits.
- Class V—qualified to fly the biggest airplanes, four-engine bombers and transports and able to deliver them overseas.

Women and men pilots would be classified the same. All ferry pilots—male and female—would carry a card stating their classifications and the planes they were qualified to ferry.

"What about the P-51?" the men asked, referring to the swift, high-powered pursuit aircraft that Nancy Love had already flown.

Colonel Tunner stuck to his guns. "The WAFS will fly everything they are capable of flying."

After April 1943, the lid was off. Women could transition into whatever they proved capable of flying. For the first time in the U.S. military, gender was not a factor.

✈ ✈ ✈

On May 1, the first twenty-three women from the Flying Training Command School in Texas reported to the Ferrying Division. They were split among the four WAFS squadrons. Overnight, the WAFS doubled in size. By early June, the number of WAFS had climbed to ninety-two with the arrival of the second class of Women's Flying Training Detachment graduates at the ferrying bases.

Colonel Tunner eyed his growing number of women pilots. He was very much aware of Jacqueline Cochran's continued activity. He needed Nancy Love, his trusted link to his women pilots, close by.

Tunner was absolutely confident of Nancy's ability to handle any situation thrust on her. He neither liked nor trusted Cochran, and with good reason as it turned out. Having Nancy at headquarters in Cincinnati to handle whatever came up was a necessity.

The Women's Flying Training Detachment, under Cochran, had been moved from Houston to Avenger Field, Sweetwater, Texas, the spring of 1943. Houston lacked the necessary facilities for training a large number of women pilots. Nancy accompanied Colonel Tunner on a visit to Avenger Field June 16. She wanted to talk to the future graduates about what to expect in the Ferrying Division.

Nancy Love instructing new pilots on what to expect on ferrying trips. *Courtesy: WASP Archive, Texas Woman's University, Denton.*

"You will have the same privileges as the officers," she told them. "You will be entitled to use the Officers Club. It is a very military life. You will learn the necessary paper work you must file when delivering an airplane. You are on duty seven days a week."

She described the ferrying trips they would make.

> The trips are long, averaging about 1,000 miles. You are completely responsible for the ship assigned to you, including having a guard on duty at night and sending an R.O.N. (Remain Over Night message) to your home base. This R.O.N. states where your ship is each night and why, so that your office knows where every ship is every day and every night.
>
> You will start on PTs and then BTs. After you fly a PT 2,000 miles cross country without a radio, you will have learned a lot about navigation. Then you will go on to AT-6s and AT-17s. It's entirely up to you and your own hard work how fast you progress.

Nancy also wrote to General Barton Yount, commanding general of the Flying Training Command, praising the graduates of the first two classes, "The flight training of the early graduates has been thorough and well adapted to their duties as ferrying pilots. Their attitude and conduct have been generally excellent."

Jackie Cochran was well aware that the women in flight training were to serve in the Ferrying Division under Nancy Love. On May 1, she sent a lengthy letter to General Arnold listing the reasons she should be in charge of the entire women's flying program.

> My own idea is that before this group of girls is militarized, they should be molded into a smooth running unit with problems relating to them in operations discovered and solved, and routines established . . . [and] when they are militarized [the Army Air Forces] should leave them a separate unit directly under the Air Force. . . . You need eyes and ears in whom you have confidence to follow this women pilot program for you. They must be experienced,

Nancy Love, Executive for WAFS, and the first aircraft she flew as a WAFS, the PT-19. *Courtesy: WASP Archive, Texas Woman's University, Denton.*

qualified eyes and ears, and they must be feminine. That's the job I would like to do, and which I think I can do well. . . . You and I had this job in mind for myself from 1941 on.

On June 28, Arnold established the Office of Special Assistant for Women Pilots and named Jacqueline Cochran Director of Women Pilots. Her duties were to decide where the women pilots could best be used and place them accordingly; establish acceptance and graduation standards; set rules of conduct; see to the women's welfare; draw up plans for militarization; and make regular inspection visits to the women's units.

Cochran's position was announced to the press July 5, 1943.

Neither the ATC nor Tunner—newly promoted to Brigadier General—was told what this announcement meant for Nancy Love and the women ferry pilots. Tunner felt the intent was to interfere with the operation of the Ferrying Division Command and its women pilots and said so. He disliked the idea of having to explain his reasons every time he found it necessary to issue orders.

To keep his command functioning smoothly, General Tunner appointed Nancy Love his Executive for WAFS. The War Department made the announcement, also on July 5.

Cochran believed her position gave her the power to administer the assignments, activities, and regulation of *all* the women pilots flying for the Army. Tunner believed it was the ATC's job to regulate its own people, and that included the groundbreaking decision to treat male and female personnel in like manner.

On August 5, the other shoe dropped when it was announced that all the Army's women pilots would now go by the name of Women Airforce Service Pilots, or WASP. The original WAFS, the WFTD graduates now serving in the Ferrying Division, twenty-five graduates Cochran recently had transferred to Camp Davis, North Carolina, and the WFTD trainees in Sweetwater all were now WASP.

"We went to bed WAFS and woke up the next morning WASP," said Betty Gillies.

Nancy Love, now spending most of her time behind a desk in Cincinnati, wondered "What next?" She described her job this way:

Nancy Love in 1943 with Alexander deSeversky, founder of the Seversky Aircraft Corporation that built the P-35. De Seversky later wrote *Victory Through Air Power*, a best-selling book about military use of aircraft. He and Nancy were good friends. She called him "Sasha." *Courtesy: The Air Power Museum, Farmingdale, Long Island.*

My duties involved administration of four WASP ferrying squadrons and planning of operational and training procedures. In addition, and this was the "fun" part, I went through transition on each type of military aircraft and ferried at least one of each kind before that particular class of airplane was released for WASP training and subsequent ferrying.

The confidence placed in Nancy Love by Generals Tunner and George was not misplaced. Nancy handled the explosion of new pilots well.

The year of the WAFS was over. The year of the WASP had begun.

Chapter Twelve

A B-17 Bound for England

GENERAL TUNNER WAS GETTING STATIC from male pilots. The men objected to ferrying B-17s to England because of the unstable weather conditions over the North Atlantic. Tunner did not consider the flights to be dangerous.

"These flights had become almost routine and there was no reason for complaint," he wrote. "So, I decided to let a couple of our girls show them just how easy it really was."

The "couple of girls" were Nancy Love and Betty Gillies.

"Our number one and number two pilots leaped at the chance to be the first women to ferry a plane overseas. We had scheduled a blitz movement of two hundred B-17s and I assigned the two women to one of those planes."

Tunner was not out to make heroines of Nancy and Betty. He knew both were skilled pilots. Already he had used women ferry pilots to prove to the men how routine most jobs in the Ferry Command could be. Two WAFS had just checked out on the challenging P-39, which the men called "the flying coffin."

In July 1943, Nancy and Betty began the biggest transition of their aviation lives—to learn to fly the four-engine B-17 Flying Fortress. Capt. Robert D. "Red" Forman was their instructor. Forman had served with Tunner since 1939.

Nancy Love and Betty Gillies begin transition to fly the B-17. *Courtesy: The Love family collection.*

Forman took Nancy and Betty through cross-country training, night flying, night landings, and operating under instrument conditions. He gave them a thorough lesson in how to fly the B-17 that included how to deal with the loss of one and two engines.

Hydraulics or no, flying the heavy Fortress was hard work, particularly when dealing with engine loss. Nancy's and Betty's endurance and physical strength were sorely tested, but they refused offers of help from Forman.

"We have to find out if we can fly this plane by ourselves," Nancy wrote to Bob.

Beginning August 18, Nancy and Betty and their crew chief, Tech Sergeant G. S. Hall, ferried a series of B-17s around the western half of the United States. By August 24, they had logged twenty-four hours of ferrying time. T/Sgt. Hall stayed with them for all their deliveries.

Both women were signed off as competent crew to fly the B-17.

On September 1, 1943, Nancy and Betty and a full four-man crew took off in the B-17 that was to take them across the cold, ominous North Atlantic.

Nancy carried a letter of introduction to Major Roy Atwood, executive officer of the ATC European Wing in London, written on official Air Transport Command letterhead. The writer asked that Atwood "receive and take care of the bearers of this letter." The letter was signed *Robert M. Love, Colonel*, with this P.S., "Incidentally one of them is my wife and the other a good friend."

The crew RONed in New Castle where they picked up the fleece-lined flight suits and oxygen masks required for the North Atlantic air route. Oxygen masks were required when flying higher than ten thousand feet. On September 3, they left for Presque Isle, Maine, the staging point for trans-Atlantic flights. They flew above solid clouds most of the way but hit clear weather 20 miles south of their destination.

General Tunner also arrived at Presque Isle that afternoon. He wanted to see his two women pilots off on their historic flight across "the Pond." The base commander and his wife threw a big dinner for the visiting dignitaries. The next morning, Nancy and Betty received their briefing and clearance and left for Goose Bay, Labrador, the last stop before heading across the North Atlantic.

Much of the trip to Goose Bay was under instrument conditions. The two WAFS stepped onto the remote, wind-swept airfield the afternoon of September 4. They would go no farther.

Gen. C. R. Smith, thinking the two women and their crew were well on their way across the Atlantic, sent a wire to the commander of the ATC European Wing.

Betty Gillies and Nancy Love after learning that General Arnold had ordered them not to fly the Atlantic. Courtesy: *The Love family collection*.

The Queen Bee crew in Goose Bay, Labrador, the morning of September 5, 1943, after General Arnold stopped the transoceanic flight. *Courtesy: The Love family collection.*

"A B-17 flown by two women pilots is on its way. Please notify General Arnold."

The telegram was delivered while the commander was having dinner with Arnold. He handed the telegram to his boss. Arnold immediately ordered the flight stopped.

> Just have seen message from C.R. Smith . . . indicating that a B-17 with women crew will leave for England shortly. . . . Desire that this trip be cancelled and no women fly transoceanic planes until I have had time to study and approve.

Word reached the crew in Goose Bay as they sat in the mess hall finishing dinner. Nancy and Betty had to step aside. The Commanding General of the United States Army Air Forces had spoken. The next morning, a photographer snapped several photos of a somber Nancy Love and Betty Gillies and their male crew standing in front of their B-17.

"We'd just been 'caught' by the higher ups and were sadly awaiting a male replacement pilot and copilot," Nancy wrote years later. "Incidentally our loyal (and brave!) male crew had named the airplane and painted 'Queen Bee' on her during the night, trying I suspect, to raise our very low morale."

Nancy and Betty boarded a C-54 as passengers the morning of September 6. The flight headed back to Presque Isle, Maine—the opposite direction from their intended destination, Prestwick, Scotland. Two male pilots took their places and ferried *Queen Bee* on to Scotland.

Chapter Thirteen

Trouble Brewing

SOON AFTER NANCY RETURNED TO CINCINNATI from the B-17 flight, Colonel Tunner and the Ferrying Division encountered a big problem with Jacqueline Cochran. Love's and Cochran's opposing views of how to organize and administer the women pilots were on a collision course.

Cochran drafted proposed regulations that would put her in charge of every phase of the WASP program, including recruitment, training, utilization, living conditions, assignment, reassignment, and discharge.

To do this, Cochran proposed to appoint and place "establishment officers," who would directly oversee squadron conduct and morale on all bases where WASP were stationed. They would report directly to the Director of Women Pilots, not to the base commander.

In October 1943, approximately 230 WASP were on active duty. Jackie Cochran had sent fifty of them to Camp Davis in North Carolina to learn to tow gunnery targets. Now under Cochran's command, they were no longer part of ATC.

The other 180 were assigned to a Ferrying Group at an ATC base, under the authority of the WASP commander, who answered to the base commander and to Nancy Love. Both the base commander and Love answered to General Tunner. Nancy had handpicked the leaders of her squadrons.

Nancy Love and her commanding officer, General William H. Tunner. *Courtesy: Author's Personal Collection.*

To Nancy, the establishment officers were little more than spies for Cochran.

General Tunner took Cochran's action as yet another attempt to wrest control of the women's squadrons from the ATC. He sent Nancy and Major Teague to Washington to draft a rebuttal.

ATC's General George approved their response and sent it to AAF Headquarters. The message read:

> The proposed regulations and organization of the WASP are a direct violation of established military chains of command, and of policies established throughout the Army Air Forces.
>
> Since it is believed that only confusion and conflict can result if this regulation is adopted, *it is the belief of this Command that it would be far better not to use WASPs in the Command than to have them operating under the proposed terms.*

Nancy Love, herself, wrote the final remark [italicized above]. ATC reminded the AAF that the WASP were civilian, not military, employees and should be treated accordingly.

None of Cochran's establishment officers were sent to ferrying bases. Tunner, Nancy, and the ATC had kept Cochran from taking control of the women's squadrons.

ATC historian Lt. Col. Oliver La Farge wrote:

> From Fall 1943 on, there was a steady push and pull between the Ferrying Division, through ATC, and Miss Cochran over the clash between ATC's sole desire to get on with its mission of delivering aircraft and training pilots, and hers to conduct a large experiment.

LaFarge also wrote in his post-war book, *The Eagle in the Egg*, "If Air Staff had only been blunter from the beginning with its

Director of Women Pilots" and emphasized the accepted military procedure, much of the conflict could have been avoided.

General Tunner did not want military control of the women ferry pilots to fall under Cochran. He made one more attempt that November to head off Cochran's efforts to interfere with the Ferrying Division. By then she and Arnold were working to militarize the WASP.

Tunner asked Nancy Love to write to Col. Oveta Culp Hobby, WAC commander. Nancy outlined Tunner's proposal for putting the WASP ferry pilots into the WAC.

Captain Walter J. Marx, the ATC historian who wrote the first history of the WASP of the Ferrying Division, documented that the letter was "pigeonholed" [stopped] by Air Staff and never reached Colonel Hobby. The Ferrying Division's request never surfaced and, consequently, was never considered.

"Plans for militarization sponsored by Miss Cochran moved on successfully," Marx wrote.

Chapter Fourteen

WASP Will Fly Pursuit

PRODUCTION OF TRAINER AIRPLANES slowed to a trickle in late summer 1943. Pursuit aircraft rolled off the factory assembly lines in ever-increasing numbers. Now General Tunner's biggest need was pilots capable of flying those high-powered fighters.

Tunner and his staff had learned that flying pursuit aircraft was an unnecessary transition step for male pilots. The men were most critically needed to fly four-engine aircraft overseas. The women *were not* going to fly overseas.

Seven original WAFS already were ferrying pursuit aircraft: Nancy Love, Betty Gillies, Helen Mary Clark, Teresa James, Del Scharr, BJ Erickson, and Evelyn Sharp. Eight more WAFS were ready to begin pursuit transition, and fifty-six women from the first three WFTD classes were close to qualifying.

Why not let the women ferry the fighter aircraft?

Tunner made his decision. On October 7, he submitted the names of the women ready to be groomed for pursuit.

Pursuit transition school opened December 1 in Palm Springs, California. Fledgling pursuit pilots, male and female, were headed there to learn to fly the four single-engine pursuits—P-47, P-40, P-39 and P-51—in a focused, four-week training period.

P-47s *Courtesy: National Museum of the US Air Force.*

P-40 *Courtesy: National Museum of the US Air Force.*

P-39 Courtesy: National Museum of the US Air Force.

P-51 Courtesy: National Museum of the US Air Force.

"The Ferrying Division saw to it that the student's instruction was the best that could be had," Iris Cummings Critchell, one of the first graduates, recalls. "Our instructors were factory reps from the manufacturers of the airplanes and the airplanes' systems. We received thorough and excellent training."

Ferrying pursuit aircraft would become the Ferrying Division's number one job by January 1944.

✈ ✈ ✈

To qualify for pursuit aircraft, a pilot had to have an instrument rating—the ability to fly blind, to safely navigate clouds and weather without visual reference to the ground. Tunner established an Instrument School in St. Joseph, Missouri, where pilots could be trained before entering Pursuit School itself.

With pursuit school on the immediate horizon, base commanders were ordered not to allow anyone to check out on pursuits on base. But Nancy soon learned that some of the Dallas women were receiving "bootleg" (illegal) transition in the P-47. Male pilots were giving the women cockpit checks without the commanding officer's knowledge. One such flight ended up in the newspapers.

Florene Miller, WAFS squadron commander at Love Field, took a P-47 aloft Sunday afternoon, November 28. When the late afternoon haze worsened, the tower told her to come in. Florene's approach was into the sun, her visibility hampered by the haze. This is Florene's account:

"As I came in, I knew exactly where I was except that I was about ten feet lower than I intended to be. I flew straight into a steel utility pole. It was strong enough that I didn't knock it down, but it made an awful, screaming metal-tearing-against metal sound. The airplane shot straight up and started to roll."

Florene had mere seconds to stabilize the stricken airplane, which she did. Then the battle to land began. Monday *Dallas Morning News* wrote:

Circling Love Field for nearly an hour at dark Sunday after the undercarriage of her heavy fighter plane sheared the power line, leaving the field in darkness [and] knocked out radio communication, Florene Miller, commander of the Women's Airforce Service Pilots, landed right side up, uninjured. Her aircraft had taken out the lights at Love Field as well as radio communications between the tower and any aircraft in the area. Through a series of emergency radio transmissions from a neighboring airfield, all the jeeps at Love Field responded and gathered along both sides of the active runway. They aimed their headlights inward. Those headlights gave Florene a lighted path. She could land between them.

November 30, Florene left for Pursuit School along with several others from Dallas.

That same day, at Long Beach, Nancy Love checked out in the twin-engine Lockheed P-38 Lightning pursuit aircraft.

She sat suspended in a narrow Plexiglas-canopied, single-seat cockpit, between and slightly above streamlined twin nacelles [the compartments that housed the two engines]. From that cockpit, Nancy had a commanding view of the Long Beach runway and taxiway complex.

This airplane was quite different from sitting in the taildragger P-51. The P-38 was equipped with the new tricycle gear. Thanks to her extensive work with Joe Gwinn's Aircar and with the Hammond Y plane, Nancy felt very much at home.

She executed the sequences in preparation for takeoff. Instead of a control stick (standard in the single-engine pursuits) the P-38 had a yoke, or a half steering wheel. To call the tower for clearance she had to press the button in the center of the yoke, which activated the microphone.

P-38 *Courtesy: National Museum of the US Air Force.*

She sat at the end of the runway, her toes pushed hard against the brakes. The airplane shook as the twin 1,475-horsepower Allison engines roared their readiness to fly. Nancy thrust twin throttles to the firewall [full on]. The Lightning surged forward, rolling faster and faster, building speed. Then, with the grace of a bird in flight, the big aircraft lifted from the runway, the ground falling away beneath its wings.

Once again, Nancy Love made history—this time as the first woman to fly the P-38.

She flew for fifty-five minutes and made two landings. On December 1, she was back for more. This time she spent two hours and twenty minutes in the air and logged five landings in the P-38.

☩ ☩ ☩

While Nancy was in Long Beach to check out in the P-38, she met Iris Cummings (Critchell), a member of BJ Erickson's squadron.

Iris vividly recalls her first meeting with the woman who commanded the WASP.

That's when I gained my appreciation for how gracefully she handled people and situations—quietly and wisely. For just a few moments, I was privileged to see her open up a bit and smile and speak warmly about flying, ferrying, and subsequently, the P-38.

She allowed herself to show her warmth and respect for BJ to those of us present. She showed the sparkle and then returned to her cool business-like bearing which served her so well.

Nancy's strength in the face of adversity was about to be tested again.

Chapter Fifteen

Pursuit School

EIGHT WOMEN AND THIRTY-FIVE MEN reported to Palm Springs November 30. They were the first class to attend the new Pursuit School. Four were Nancy Love's original WAFS—Dorothy Scott, Florene Miller, Helen Richards, and Gertrude Meserve—and four were early WFTD graduates stationed in Dallas.

Nancy Love wanted to wish them well. She also needed to talk to Florene and get her side of that fateful P-47 flight. On December 3, she left Long Beach flying the P-38 to Palm Springs, ninety miles as the crow flies, through the pass between the imposing 10,000-foot twin peaks of California's San Jacinto Mountain.

She expected to return later that afternoon. That didn't happen.

In Palm Springs, Nancy and Florene met on the flight line where aircraft waiting to be flown were parked. Florene later recalled that the two of them waved to Dorothy Scott as she and her instructor climbed into a BC-1 [AT-6] trainer. Florene was next in line to fly the BC-1.

A high thin overcast limited the visibility to thirty miles. The desert temperature was a pleasant 76 degrees, and the wind was four miles per hour out of the west-northwest. The sun was low in the southwest and cast long shadows. Scott entered her final approach, establishing a normal gliding attitude. Above and behind her, a P-39 also swung into its final approach.

WAFS Dorothy Scott. *Courtesy: The Dorothy Scott family collection.*

The student pilot in the P-39 could not see Scott's plane because of the position of the low winter sun and the angle of his aircraft's descent. He was above her and descending faster than she was.

The control tower shouted a warning, but it came too late. The P-39 came down over the trainer. The two planes collided in mid-air. The tail section of the BC-1 was severed. Both ships crashed into the ground and the BC-1 burst into flames upon impact.

Scott died, as did her instructor and the P-39 pilot.

Dorothy had been Nancy Love's copilot on a recent C-47 delivery. They established the beginnings of a friendship during that trip. Nancy was impressed with Dorothy's abilities, her passion for flying, and her gung-ho attitude. She also remembered meeting Dorothy and her father when they arrived in Wilmington by automobile, November 1942, all the way from Washington State.

Now she recalled Dorothy's earnest face, her absolute dedication to flying, her youth, and her promise. No one can know what Nancy went through in private. As with Cornelia's death, she hid her emotions from the public and worked through her anguish in private.

Two of Nancy's original WAFS had died, both in mid-air collisions, but in neither case was the woman pilot at fault. There was no question of pilot error on Scott's part. The blame was assigned to the control tower.

The accident report concluded that the camouflaged aircraft used in Palm Springs contributed to the crash and recommended that all aircraft used in Pursuit Transition be painted yellow. Other contributing factors were late afternoon haze, low slanting sunlight, and deep shadows.

Nancy did not attend Dorothy's funeral. That day, December 6, she flew to Dallas to check into Florene's accident.

The Dorothy Scott tragedy, only days after Florene's accident, could put the women's program at risk. But for Florene's safe landing of the damaged P-47, Nancy could have lost two pilots in less than a week. She feared a decision from higher up would halt women's transition into pursuits.

Nancy had the reputation of her women pilots to uphold. If, because of two back-to-back accidents, questions were raised about the women's fitness to fly pursuit, her hard work could come tumbling down around her. The less ruckus raised, the less attention called to the incident, the better.

Florene had disobeyed orders. According to Army procedure, Nancy relieved her of her command in Dallas, placed Delphine Bohn in charge of the 5th Ferrying Group's WASP squadron, and transferred Florene to Long Beach. The women ferry pilots continued to do their job, and women pilots continued to be assigned to pursuit school.

On December 14, having completed her investigation of Florene's accident on General Tunner's orders, Nancy wrote to him:

> [I recommend] that no quota for pursuit school be required of any WASP squadron. When a pilot is judged by transition to be superior, every effort should be made to give her an instrument course and to make her a thoroughly competent Class III pilot, after which she should be sent to pursuit school. Pilots who are judged borderline cases should be given further ferrying duties until such time as their ability is considered sufficient to fly more complicated aircraft.

The Ferrying Division needed all the qualified pursuit pilots it could find, but not every WASP—not even every original WAFS—wanted to fly pursuit.

Nancy did not think a woman should be compelled to fly pursuit if she didn't want to. WAFS pilots were not military. They were civilians not covered by military insurance or any other military benefits. They were on their own.

But knowing the need for pursuit pilots, she made an eloquent plea to the Ferrying Group commanders to encourage their WASP ferry pilots to work toward qualifying for pursuit school. They were badly needed. She reminded the men that women pilots now were allowed unlimited opportunity for advancement.

To her women pilots, Nancy wrote, "Those WASP who are capable of flying these types will be performing the greatest service for their country and for the Ferrying Division."

Delphine Bohn and the P-38 Lightning. *Courtesy: Delphine Bohn Collection, History of Aviation Collection, Special Collections and Archives Division, Eugene McDermott Library, The University of Texas at Dallas.*

By April 1, 1944, twenty-seven women had graduated from pursuit school in Palm Springs. The first flight each of those newly minted pursuit pilots made was to pick up a P-51 from the North American Aviation factory in Inglewood, California, and ferry it to Newark, New Jersey, the gateway to the Atlantic and the war.

Pursuit school was moved to Brownsville, Texas, in April 1944. Ninety-six more women would graduate, including one more of Nancy's original WAFS, Sis Bernheim. Sis graduated on July 15, and immediately was assigned to ferry P-47s from Farmingdale, Long Island, to Newark.

Chapter Sixteen

The Quest for Militarization

WHY MILITARIZE THE WOMEN PILOTS?

Military status would give the WASP military insurance, death benefits, hospitalization insurance, and pensions. Time served in the WASP would be counted toward retirement and benefits, should any of these women later enter government service in other areas.

By 1944, the country's mood toward the war had changed. Uncertainty fell away as the military might of the United States began to roll forward.

General Arnold had overestimated the number of pilots needed to win the war. Pilot casualties had been far fewer than anticipated. On January 15, 1944, he terminated the flight-training program for new male pilots. This action put several hundred civilian flight instructors out of work. Those men also lost their draft deferment status, making them eligible to be drafted for "the walking Army." The young men waiting in line for those now cancelled flight-training classes also were now prime candidates for the draft.

The aftershock from Arnold's decision to end the flight-training program would bring the WASP program to its knees.

Nancy Love called a meeting of her WASP squadron commanders at her headquarters in Cincinnati in early January. Discussion of plans and changes for the upcoming year was the agenda. The biggest potential change hanging over all of them was the probability that the Arnold-Cochran plan for militarization would be approved and Nancy had chosen not to fight it. The group avoided any discussion of this topic.

Her squadron commanders were unanimous in their opposition. None of them wanted to be militarized under Cochran.

BJ Erickson (Long Beach), Delphine Bohn (Dallas), and Betty Gillies (Wilmington) wanted to find out if they could join the Army Air Forces the same way civilian male ferry pilots did. The process was simple, sign up as individuals, begin ferrying aircraft, and after a specified number of months served, the men were commissioned in the USAAF.

When the meeting in Cincinnati was over, Erickson, Bohn, and Gillies traveled to Washington. There, they learned that militarization of the WASP, as a group, was now a top military priority. That didn't stop them from trying for a USAAF commission. They met with several military men they thought could help them. They also spoke with several high-ranking WAC (Women's Army Corps) officers. But their hopes of joining the AAF as individual ferry pilots were dashed. It wasn't going to happen.

In the meantime, Nancy Love learned that three of her trusted lieutenants were snooping around Washington, stirring things up.

Nancy knew she had to put a stop to it. The Arnold-Cochran militarization had gone too far, and the personal futures of her women ferry pilots could be at risk. She telephoned them and, as Delphine later wrote, "she very gently, but very firmly, ordered us back to our bases." Thus ended the only grassroots attempt by the women ferry pilots to militarize.

Meanwhile, Congressman John Costello of California had introduced the bill calling for the militarization of the WASP in fall 1943. The amended version, H.R. (House of Representatives) 4219, was submitted to Congress in February 1944.

Barbara "BJ" Erickson. *Courtesy: The Barbara Erickson London family collection.*

Delphine Bohn. *Courtesy: The Dorothy Scott family collection.*

Betty Gillies. *Courtesy: WASP Archive, Texas Woman's University, Denton*

Nancy Love in her Santiago blue WASP uniform. *Courtesy: The Air Power Museum, Farmingdale, Long Island.*

When word of House Bill 4219 reached the streets through the nation's newspapers, Congress began to receive angry protests from the civilian flying instructors now out of jobs and threatened with the draft. The American Legion and other veterans' organizations joined in the protest. As did mothers of boys who had been transferred from the cancelled aviation cadet training status to the infantry.

Congress showed far more interest in the plight of the young male trainees and the out-of-work instructors than in a handful of women pilots. The anti-WASP forces made a lot of noise. The politicians paid attention, proving that the squeaky wheel gets the grease.

Amid this contention, hearings on the WASP bill began in March 1944.

The bill said that for the duration of the war, women would be commissioned as flight officers or aviation students in accordance with existing regulations. No woman would be appointed to a grade above colonel and there would be no more than one officer of that grade. Female flight cadets, upon successful completion of the prescribed course of training, would be commissioned as second lieutenants in the Army of the United States. All commissioned women would receive the same pay and allowances as male members of the Army and they would be entitled to the same rights, privileges, and benefits according to their rank, grade, and length of service.

✈ ✈ ✈

Nancy Love, Jackie Cochran, and her deputy, Ethel Sheehy, flanked General Arnold when he testified for the WASP before the friendly House Armed Services Committee. All three women were smartly dressed in their spiffy new WASP uniforms.

The Committee heard Arnold out, then asked for a closed-door session. General Arnold was the only witness heard. The three women were not allowed to observe. The Committee gave the WASP Bill a "favorable" recommendation for passage when it reached the House of Representatives.

However, because the WASP were classified under Civil Service, public funds were being spent on them. The men in Congress knew next to nothing about the women or the program and decided that they needed to know how the money was being spent. The House Committee on Civil Service, led by Georgia Congressman Robert J. Ramspeck, decided to investigate.

Nancy Love was one of several individuals the committee called to be deposed, which means she'd answer questions under oath, about the WASP program and how the government's money was being spent. The Committee was *not* concerned about using women pilots. Its concern was the recruiting of inexperienced personnel and the money being spent on the program.

Congressional debate on militarization continued and the anti-WASP press coverage became increasingly more hostile until the bill finally came to a vote in the House of Representatives on June 21, 1944.

Chapter Seventeen

The Women in Pursuit

BY 1944, FERRYING PURSUIT AIRCRAFT was the number-one priority of the women assigned to Nancy Love's squadrons.

Betty Gillies sent her first eight pursuit-qualified pilots to the Republic Aviation factory on Long Island where the heavily armored P-47 pursuit aircraft were built. From the factory, it was a mere half-hour flight to the docks at Newark, New Jersey—fifty miles west. There, the planes were loaded onto Liberty ships bound for England.

The close proximity of the factory to those docks meant that, if blessed with good weather, each woman could move several airplanes in one day.

To make that happen, Betty requested the permanent use of a twin-engine C-60 transport plane from her base commander in Wilmington. In the C-60, a WASP pilot and copilot could follow the pursuit aircraft to Newark. Once the fighters were delivered, the pursuit pilots climbed aboard the big transport. Their sister pilots in the cockpit flew them all back to Farmingdale.

The presence of the C-60 spared six P-47 pilots from the time-consuming process of making their way across Manhattan Island and back to Long Island by ground transportation. Once the C-60 delivered them to Farmingdale, those six could immediately climb into another P-47 and fly it to Newark.

Three of Nancy Love's Originals—Nancy Batson, Gertrude Meserve, and Teresa James—traded off flying the C-60 and ferrying the P-47s.

The pilots from Betty's command were so good at what they did that, as of June 8, 1944, they took over all the ferrying out of the Republic factory. The male ferry pilots were assigned elsewhere.

When the Romulus-based pilots returned from pursuit school, they went to work ferrying Curtiss P-40s out of Buffalo and P-39s [replaced later by P-63s] out of the Bell plant in Niagara Falls, New York. Those were delivered to Great Falls, Montana, where male ferry pilots took them on to Alaska to be handed over to Russian pilots. Providing planes to the Russians was made possible by the Lend Lease Act, which was enacted in March 1941 and in force throughout the war.

The WASP squadrons at both Long Beach and Dallas were close to North American Aviation factories that produced the P-51s. The women flew the Mustangs to Newark, the gateway to the Atlantic and to the war in Europe.

As more and more women qualified as pursuit pilots, they joined in these deliveries. The ferry pilots were so busy, they rarely had a day off.

✛ ✛ ✛

After Dorothy Scott's death at pursuit school, Nancy Love spent the winter trouble-shooting for Tunner. Misunderstandings of what the women were and were not allowed to fly dated back to March 1943. The reaction to Cornelia Fort's fatal accident continued to dictate caution in the minds of some senior officers.

Women ferry pilots still were being kept out of the cockpits of airplanes they needed to fly in order to qualify for pursuit school. General Tunner assigned Nancy to set the record straight on WASP transition and the planes they could fly. General Tunner, himself, tried to motivate his Group commanders with this letter:

C-60. *Courtesy: National Museum of the US Air Force.*

It is desired to progress qualified WASP as rapidly as possible consistent with safe practice, so that they may be eligible for Pursuit School. Copilot training will expedite transition on Class III and Class IV aircraft. You are reminded that you are authorized to assign WASP co-pilots with male pilots on delivery flights. It is desired that this practice be instituted after careful consultation with your WASP Squadron Leader.

Every WASP willing to go to pursuit school was asked to sign a statement saying that pursuit school was her choice *before* she was given the prerequisite Class III transition and instrument training.

Pursuits were swift and powerful and could be unforgiving of a pilot's mistakes. This made them dangerous to fly. Pursuit crashes had already taken the lives of several male pilots. It was only a matter of time before a woman pilot would die at the controls.

The P-51 was the Long Beach WASP's major responsibility but following Nancy Love's checkout in the twin-engine Lockheed P-38,

Evelyn Sharp. *Courtesy: The Barbara Erickson London family collection.*

Betty Gillies and BJ Erickson had checked out in the Lightning. Evelyn Sharp was next.

Evelyn was a quick study and a proven pilot. Twenty-three when she joined the WAFS in 1942, she already had logged an impressive 2,968 hours. She was checked out and on March 30, she took off in a new P-38, destination Newark.

† † †

She spent the first night in Palm Springs, the second night in Amarillo, then on to Cincinnati April 1 to meet with Nancy Love. Evelyn was scheduled to take command of a new WASP ferrying squadron starting up in Palm Springs. The two needed to talk strategy.

The following day Evelyn headed for Newark, but landed at New Cumberland, Pennsylvania, near Harrisburg. She decided to RON there because of bad weather over the Allegheny Mountains. The next morning, April 3, she climbed into the cockpit, settled herself down in the seat, and began the engine run-up and pre-takeoff cockpit check.

When she was cleared for takeoff, she turned onto the narrow runway, lined the nosewheel up in the center, and pushed the throttle to full forward. She was wheels up at 10:29.

Black smoke poured from the left engine. The P-38 stalled and, for a split second, hung in the air. The left-wing tip dipped and caught a cluster of trees. The sleek silver aircraft hit the ground flat, skidded ten feet, and stopped.

The Plexiglas canopy lay upside down a few feet in front of the right propeller. The clock on the instrument panel read 10:30. Evelyn died instantly.

Three of Nancy Love's WAFS—Cornelia, Dorothy and Evelyn—had died in service to their country.

Chapter Eighteen

Officer Training School

GENERAL TUNNER NO LONGER HAD sufficient trainer-type airplanes for lesser-qualified WASP to ferry. In April 1944, he told Love and Cochran to work out the transfer of the pilots not qualified to fly pursuit back to the Training Command for reassignment.

Cochran had succeeded in securing Officer Training School (OTS) for the WASP in anticipation of their militarization. As a member of the first class, Nancy was due in Orlando, Florida, April 19. Her deposition with the Ramspeck Committee was scheduled the prior Sunday.

Knowing Nancy was coming to Washington, Cochran invited her to be a weekend houseguest at her D.C. apartment. There, they began a series of WASP reassignments that would occupy the time and energy of both women over the next four months.

Wilmington and Long Beach no longer had trainer aircraft to ferry. Nancy and Jackie gave Tunner the names of forty women to be transferred to non-ferrying bases.

On April 16, representatives of the Ramspeck Committee interviewed Nancy.

Afterward, she typed a report of the questions she was asked and her answers.

Q. What do you think of the qualifications of the girls who come from the training school [Avenger Field, Sweetwater, Texas]?
A. They are good pilots. They are on a par with what I know of the male graduates of the Training Command.
Q. What is the policy on pursuit pilots?
A. We need pursuit pilots.
Q. (He) was very interested in the relationship between Miss Cochran and myself. Wanted to know if there was a battle between us.
A. (I said) Miss Cochran's was an administrative job and mine was an operational one, and there was no battle between us.
Q. Do the girls want militarization?
A. The majority do.
Q. Why do the girls want to be militarized?
A. For recognition and protection. A civilian girl going into a modification center to pick up an airplane is open to suspicion as a spy. Also, compensation and insurance for the families would then be available to them.
Q. How much do you think, off the record, that the uniform is worth?
A. I have no idea. I have never been interested in clothes.
Q. What items are issued and what are purchased?
A. We are issued two winter and two summer uniforms. We purchase accessories, etc.
Q. What is the pay of the other operational WAFS?
A. $250 per month, plus overtime, which comes to about $280.
Q. Who are the girls who are competing for the Air Medal?
A. I have no idea what you mean. It has been awarded to Miss Erickson.
Q. How did she make those deliveries so fast?
A. The weather was good; she is a good pilot and a hard worker; and she had fast airplanes.

WASP at Officer Training School in Orlando. *Courtesy: Author's Personal Collection, gift of Nancy Batson Crews.*

Following her meetings with Cochran and the Ramspeck Committee, Nancy flew to Orlando.

The first OTS class included several other Originals—Gillies, Batson, Donahue, Erickson, Bohn, Miller, Batten, and Scharr—as well as Training School graduates who had been on active duty the longest. A new class would begin the first and third Wednesday of every month.

Nancy Love focused on pulling down the top score in the class. As the executive officer, she felt she had to, and she succeeded. The curriculum consisted of military discipline, courtesy and customs, chemical warfare, and the organization of the army and staff procedures.

The timing couldn't have been worse. The war's biggest movement of pursuit aircraft so far was in process, and the Ferrying Division desperately needed every pursuit ferry pilot it could lay its hands on to move those airplanes. It could not afford even the temporary loss of a dozen or more of its best pilots. Though the women didn't know it, D-Day, the decisive invasion of Europe at Normandy, France, was a few weeks away.

The WASP program and the fate of the women pilots was now being debated daily in the press. Meanwhile, the women sent to Florida were learning to be officers.

Nancy Love and the other women pilots had several visitors in Orlando—columnists from East Coast newspapers among them. Jacqueline Cochran flew in to greet the first class and invited Nancy, Betty Gillies, Delphine Bohn, and others to dinner. Another who called on the attendees was Congressman Robert Ramspeck, himself.

"He invited Nancy Love and three or four of us to have dinner with him, all the while he queried us as to the WASP," Delphine later wrote.

The Originals weren't too keen on being militarized under "Colonel" Jacqueline Cochran. The WAFS resented Cochran, feeling she had interfered with their mission and taken away the command Nancy Love was entitled to.

Chapter Nineteen

Militarization Denied

ON JUNE 5, 1944, the Ramspeck Committee presented its report to Congress. The WASP program, the report said, was "unnecessary and unjustifiably expensive." The committee opposed WASP militarization and recommended that "the recruiting of inexperienced women and their training as pilots be terminated immediately."

On June 6, D-Day, Allied troops landed on the beaches at Normandy, France, and began the push that would end the war in Europe eleven months later.

On June 21, Congress voted down WASP Bill 4219. Militarization was denied by 19 votes. Five days later, General Arnold announced that recruitment and training of additional WASP would cease. No new classes would begin after July 1. Young women already on their way to Sweetwater for that class were sent home.

The WASP operations would continue, and the women on active duty would continue to serve. The women in training at Avenger Field would be allowed to graduate and be assigned to active duty.

Jackie Cochran, ATC's General George, and three other generals were asked to make recommendations as to the future of the WASP program.

✢ ✢ ✢

Nancy Love calls Headquarters from the Orlando Airport during OTC training. *Courtesy: The Love family collection.*

What was called "The Great Transfer"—the movement of non-pursuit-qualified WASP from the Ferry Command back to the Training Command for reassignment—was in the works.

In an early July telephone conversation between Nancy Love and Jackie Cochran, the topic was the transfer of 126 WASP. But first, the two leaders had to act quickly to stop the Training Command from sending 15 new Avenger graduates to Ferrying Division squadrons. To avoid confusion and added expense, it was best that they be sent directly to their newly assigned bases.

"Do you have all the girls you'll ever want, or do you have too many now?" Cochran asked.

"We can use more if they're qualified," Nancy answered. "We have sixty-nine qualified on pursuit and twelve more just graduated."

The 15 graduates of Class 44-4, May 23, were the last sent to the Ferrying Division. One of them, former flight instructor Maurine Miller, did become a pursuit pilot. She had the hours and soon the qualifications for Pursuit School. She graduated October 1, 1944, in the next-to-last pursuit class attended by WASP. She was sent to Romulus where she ferried P-63s to Great Falls throughout the final three months of her WASP service.

On August 15, 1944, the Ferrying Division released 126 of its women pilots, roughly half of those then actively serving, for reassignment.

WASP Byrd Granger wrote in *On Final Approach:* "[Some] historical reports attempt to make it appear that the girls who were transferred out of the Ferrying Division in August 1944 were unqualified or inexperienced or unsuited for the work for which they were trained. [The] . . . ferrying of trainer type airplanes was falling off rapidly . . . women pilots would be utilized almost altogether in pursuit work. . . . This lack of qualification in many cases was due only to lack of time to gain flying experience."

BJ Erickson London, WASP squadron leader in Long Beach, echoed that assessment. "The transfer the summer of 1944 was very simple. The girls who had not qualified in pursuits were sent back to the Training Command. We had no other airplanes left for them to fly. By sending them to other assignments, they got to fly airplanes they were qualified to fly, doing other jobs at other bases."

After the Great Transfer, the Ferrying Division averaged about 140 women pilots, less than half the highest number, 303, that it had reached in early April. Eighteen of Nancy Love's Originals were still ferrying, 14 of them flying the badly needed pursuit aircraft.

General William H. Tunner. *Courtesy: National Museum of the US Air Force.*

Chapter Twenty

Tunner is Transferred

NANCY LOVE HAD KNOWN FOR SOME TIME that General Tunner was to be reassigned. He had been her personal mentor and a determined advocate of the women ferry pilots. Who would replace him, she wondered, and how would this affect her and her women pilots?

On August 1, 1944, Tunner left Cincinnati to take command of ATC's strategic Hump Operation halfway around the world that covered three Asian nations—China, Burma, and India. Before he left, he wrote a glowing commendation for Nancy:

> I wish to express my appreciation for the loyal, devoted, and cooperative efforts, which you have put forth in the interests of the Ferrying Division since 12 March 1942.

Nancy had "organized and then supervised the WAFS, for which there was no precedent in military annals," Tunner pointed out. He concluded with:

> You have dependably and efficiently performed every assignment given you. Your splendid service and your loyalty have been a source of deep satisfaction to me.

Tunner's unwavering support had been key to Nancy's ability to achieve success with women pilots and the women's ferrying program as a whole.

On August 1, 1944, Cochran submitted her report addressing the failure of the militarization bill and the termination of the WASP training school program. She recommended to General Arnold that the women pilots either be militarized or "serious consideration should be given to inactivation of the WASP program."

Putting the WASP in the WAC, she said, was not acceptable. That had been her stance from the beginning. On the contrary, the Ferrying Division and Nancy Love had no objection to its women pilots becoming part of the Women's Army Corps.

WASP Class 44-6 graduated three days later. The women were assigned to duties around the country, but none were assigned to the Ferrying Division. The women in WASP classes 44-7 through 44-10 continued to train at Sweetwater, graduate, and be assigned to active duty.

The remaining women ferry pilots continued to ferry P-47s, P-51s, P-38s, P-63s, [they had replaced P-39s], and A-20s to embarkation points to be shipped overseas. Later in the fall, five of the most experienced WASP checked out in and ferried the new twin-engine P-61 Black Widow. A night fighter, it carried radar equipment that allowed the crew to locate and attack enemy aircraft in total darkness.

Betty Gillies, Nancy's second-in-command, was the first woman to fly the P-61. The manufacturer Northrup, like so many aircraft companies, was located in the LA basin. Four WASP from nearby Long Beach—BJ Erickson, Iris Cummings, Ginny Hill, and Katy Loft—ferried several P-61s late in 1944. No P-61 flights are recorded in Nancy's logbook.

The women also ferried war-weary aircraft to any of several graveyards around the country. This was considered hazardous duty. Many of the aircraft had been damaged in combat and were badly shot up.

Nancy and BJ were assigned to deliver a battle-scarred B-17 to a mechanics school in Amarillo, Texas.

The aircraft had been affectionately nicknamed *Genevieve* by its first repair crew and the men asked to be notified of her fate. Reading further in the aircraft's official logbook, Nancy and BJ discovered her impressive combat record. *Genevieve* had performed honorably in the war over Europe.

Their entire trip was flown at reduced speed with the inoperable landing gear locked in the down position. This significantly slowed their cross-country airspeed. Oil leaked from the engines, which periodically gave off explosive noises. In order to make it to Amarillo, *Genevieve* had to have extensive repairs at both of its en route stops.

Nevertheless, Nancy, BJ, and *Genevieve's* loyal flight engineer, nicknamed "Swamp Root," lovingly delivered the weary lady to her final resting place.

"We became very fond of her," Nancy wrote later. "We felt a certain spiritual kinship with her, since we share a common and ignominious fate, we being bound for our grave—figuratively speaking—when the WASP are inactivated."

✛ ✛ ✛

The tides of war were shifting. On August 24, Allied troops recaptured Paris, setting off a celebration on both sides of the Atlantic. [Paris had been captured and held by the Germans since June 14, 1940.]

Early in September, Nancy Love was feeling wrung out. She had been ill with the flu. Once recovered, she went to Dallas to fill in for her ailing squadron commander, Delphine Bohn.

Delphine was the third Original WAFS to be sidelined by pneumonia that summer. The first, Dorothy Fulton, was so ill she was given a medical discharge. Esther Manning was next. Her recovery was slow, but she returned, only to resign in October.

Dorothy Fulton. *Courtesy: Harriet Fulton Parker, Dorothy's sister.*

Nancy wrote to Delphine, who was recuperating at her mother's house in Amarillo:

> The WASP situation remains in its usual SNAFU state, but I've acquired a new slant on it, and have tried to transmit same to the gals, i.e., we are now the long-sought-for, small select group. We've got a heck of a good record behind us and an even rosier one ahead, or should have with this bunch of good pilots. So forget the newspapers, the Training Command, J.C., WTS/CAA and the whole damned mess—and fly!

Esther Manning (Rathfelder). *Courtesy: Author's Personal Collection.*

If the WASP are abolished, we're still civilian pilots, and darned good ones. Though I've outgrown optimism in the last two years, I have it on pretty good authority that we who are left in the Ferrying Division are not to worry, but to keep mouths shut, eyes on the ball, stop arguing and fly the pants off any and all airplanes assigned to us—from L2s . . . to A-20s or B-17s.

We've all gotten so violent about this that I think it's broken down our health. So let's stop worrying, have fun, and see what happens.

Nancy—you know, POLLYANNA—Love.

On September 29, OTS was discontinued. Four-hundred-sixty WASP had completed the course, but the military standing they had expected to receive had been denied.

On October 2, General Arnold revealed the total casualties suffered by the Army Air Forces since the outbreak of the war. They were far fewer than the numbers for which the Army had planned. Now the AAF had all the pilots it needed for anticipated combat assignments.

The following day, Arnold made public his decision that the WASP would be disbanded on December 20, 1944.

Chapter Twenty-one

Closing Down

GENERAL TUNNER'S REPLACEMENT, Gen. Robert E. Nowland, was totally supportive of the women flyers. And Tunner's transfer turned out to be a blessing in disguise for Bob and Nancy Love.

The war put a tremendous strain on marriages. Bob and Nancy Love were no different from the countless other couples who had to endure long separations and great uncertainty. Their wartime logbooks show occasions when they spent even an abbreviated amount of time together were rare.

Bob's wartime letters to Nancy voiced three major concerns: he did not like living apart from his wife; it bothered him that Nancy let Cochran upset her; prior to the defeat of WASP militarization in Congress, he was concerned about her interest in a military career that wasn't there before the war.

In wartime, there wasn't much the Loves could do about living apart. As for dealing with Cochran, Nancy was not prone to public temper flare-ups. That cool control, the proper conduct for a lady learned from her mother, took over. But she did vent her frustration to Bob. Self-control and keeping those kinds of feelings private was extremely important to her.

To deal with the long separations from his wife, Bob began lobbying for reassignment to be near her. When General Tunner left for India, Bob, who had lived with five other ATC officers in Washington, D.C., since Nancy went to Wilmington in July 1942, got his wish.

When General Nowland was named commander of the Ferrying Division, Col. Robert M. Love became his deputy commander. On August 31, 1944, Bob left for Cincinnati. He wrote **"PERM CHANGE STA!"** in bold cap letters in his logbook when he landed in Cincinnati to stay. He and Nancy were together again.

Bob had been offered a Douglas, twin-engine A-20 for his personal use. When he left for a three-week fact-finding trip to South America for the ATC, he left the A-20 in Cincinnati for Nancy to fly, and she made the most of it.

"It's a stripped-down G model," she wrote after the war, "sensitive on the controls, and a spirited personality all of its own." While Bob was in South America, Nancy logged fourteen cross-country trips in the A-20 visiting her squadrons. It became her plane until the WASP were deactivated.

Letters from Cochran and Arnold were delivered on October 8, and the WASP learned that they would be disbanded and when. They were stunned. Their work, however, was not finished. For the women in the Ferrying Division, the pace had picked up. They were constantly on the go.

"Production was so heavy that we frequently had rows of P-51s stored in the middle of the Long Beach Airport," BJ Erickson London recalled. "If you got back to base by noon, Operations sent you right back out that day. You picked up the airplane and headed for Palm Springs. The following morning you headed east."

Delivering the P-51s was *the* priority. After delivery to Newark, the women returned to base as quickly as possible.

"At the Newark airport where we landed, the harbor was right there. The ships were waiting for our airplanes," Iris Cummings Critchell recalls. "When we landed, the men were in such a hurry,

Jean Landis ready to ferry a P-51. *Courtesy: Jean Landis.*

they'd start to pull the P-51 by the tail to be loaded—with us still in the cockpit! They wanted them on their way to England or Italy as fast as possible."

Because of the necessity of returning to base so they could ferry yet another aircraft, ferry pilots had government priority allowing them first access to seats on airliners. Once the planes were delivered at Newark, the pilots were shuttled through the city's traffic to La Guardia Airport by the women of the New York City Red Cross. There, they caught commercial airliners back to base.

By September 1944, the women pilots in the Ferrying Division were ferrying three-fifths of all the pursuit aircraft coming off the assembly lines. Forty-nine percent of the pilots ferrying pursuit aircraft were WASP. Men were being sent overseas as soon as they could be released from other duties.

General Nowland wrote to General Arnold on November 1, 1944, to point out problems that would be encountered by the Ferrying Division when the women pilots were let go. He offered a dollars-spent estimate on what replacing the women ferry pilots would cost. He asked that he be allowed to keep the women until their male replacements could be trained and brought on duty. He would then let the women go gradually.

Arnold told Nowland, "Inactivation of the WASP was based on a policy decision which has a vital effect upon the AAF as a whole. Evaluation of this program in terms of dollars and cents is not the immediate issue at stake and personnel under your control should scrupulously avoid any discussion along this line."

Base commanders around the country were not happy about losing their WASP pilots. The WASP performed their jobs well. Nancy and Jackie and the WASP had proved that women pilots could do the job.

Why were the WASP shut down? Contrary to rumors, it was not because Nancy Love and Jackie Cochran had fundamental differences on how the organization should be run. Nor was it because Cochran asked Arnold either to militarize the WASP or shut them down.

It was a practical matter. In spite of the fact that the WASP ferry pilots were delivering airplanes as fast as possible, what mattered was, the Allies were winning the war. Disbanding the WASP became the sensible thing to do.

Army historians tell it this way:

> To the casual observer, unacquainted with the course of military events the summer of 1944, the AAF would appear to have made an about-face on the WASP question.
> In June, General Arnold was pleading for the induction of women pilots into the Army as a military necessity.

In October [when the WASP were officially notified of their deactivation] he was stating that unless the program was deactivated these pilots would be keeping men out of the air.

The explanation for this rapid change in view apparently lies in the phenomenal military successes of the intervening months [June through September] and in an AAF attrition rate much lower than had been expected. [*The Army Air Forces in World War II, Vol. VI: Men and Planes.* Craven and Cates, eds.]

Scholar Molly Merryman writes in *Clipped Wings:* "Perhaps the most important factor leading to the demise of the Women Airforce Service Pilots program was a negative media campaign precipitated in part by the return of combat pilots from overseas and the release of Army Air Forces cadets and pilot trainers into the 'walking Army' for service in anticipated large-scale ground assaults against Japan's military." The men wanted the WASP's jobs.

Another reason may have been that America wasn't used to seeing women in roles traditionally associated with men.

Nancy Love was not blind to these realities. She knew some male pilots were prone to easily deflated egos and were looking for cases of favoritism. They claimed WASP got better assignments.

Nancy "did all that was possible to counteract male pilot antagonism," ATC historian Captain Marx wrote, "first by seeing that the girls did a thorough job and without fanfare and secondly by deliberately avoiding occasions that might lead to antagonism." On occasion, she even protested when General Tunner asked for women to be placed on assignments that might arouse jealousy among some male pilots.

Of course, it wasn't enough.

Nancy Love and Bea Medes, pilot and copilot, in a C-54. *Courtesy: The Love family collection.*

Chapter Twenty-two

Nancy Flies the Big One

LATE IN NOVEMBER Nancy Love checked out on and then ferried several Douglas four-engine C-54 transports, the biggest airplane she had ever flown. She later wrote about the experience, "This was fun. There were always large numbers of hopeful military personnel thumbing their way on leave or change-of-station and my WASP copilot and I filled the plane on every trip. Playing airline pilot fulfilled another of my ambitions!"

On Nancy's first C-54 delivery, the plane carried seventy-two passengers and a black puppy from San Francisco to New York's La Guardia. The plane was the first C-54 (the civilian model was called the DC-4) to be delivered to American Export Airlines. The chief pilot and many company officials were at the field at 1 p.m., awaiting its arrival. Nancy later recalled:

> They had never had such a big one before and were much impressed by the size of the plane. They hurried aboard, walked up the long passenger aisle, opened the front cockpit door with expressions of triumph and welcome on their faces.
>
> They stopped in a sort of frozen shock as their minds finally grasped the fact that the two happily grinning pilots were—women! Without a word, they turned and walked out again.

The Last Supper, New Castle AAB, December 16, 1944. *Courtesy: Author's Personal Collection, gift of Nancy Batson Crews.*

The women of the Training Command reached out to Nancy. She was invited to attend the final graduation ceremonies at Avenger Field, scheduled to take place December 7. She chose not to go and wrote on her invitation, "*No* answer as far as I'm concerned. NHL."

Was it shortsighted of Nancy not to attend? Probably, but she was, by then, at the end of her energy, as were most of the women ferry pilots. As she had told Delphine Bohn earlier, "I've outgrown optimism."

Nancy was not a joiner. She also opted not to join the Order of Fifinella, formed by Houston and Sweetwater graduates to keep track of each other and in the hope of holding reunions.

The Originals followed Nancy's example. They still resented being placed under Cochran's authority. And they resented giving up the WAFS uniforms they had worn with such pride. In their opinion, had Cochran not meddled in the work they were doing for the Ferrying Division, they would not be looking at deactivation and the loss of their jobs.

Had they remained a squadron of 50 women ferry pilots—as originally anticipated—and had they not encountered Cochran's

The WASP Ferry Pilots, New Castle AAB. *Courtesy: Author's Personal Collection, gift of Nancy Batson Crews.*

interference, it is likely they would have continued to serve at least until the war in Europe was over.

Nancy's final flight as a WASP was December 14-15, 1944. Her WASP copilot was Bea Medes who had spent nearly all of 1944 as Nancy's indispensable secretary. The two left the Douglas plant in Chicago to deliver C-54B #42-72389 to the West Coast.

On December 16, the Wilmington WASP of the 2nd Ferrying Group gathered at the NCAAB Officers Club for what that group christened "The Last Supper." Nancy returned for the occasion. Eight Original WAFS sat at the head table with Betty Gillies and Nancy Love in the center. All were dressed in their Santiago blue WASP uniform jackets and skirts. To Nancy's right were Nancy Batson, Helen McGilvery, and Gertrude Meserve Tubbs. To Betty's left were her executive officer Helen Mary Clark, Teresa James, and Sis Bernheim. The rest of the squadron, thirty graduates of Houston or Sweetwater, sat at tables on each side of the head table.

What went through Nancy's head that night? She had created a small cadre of dedicated professional pilots, who had volunteered to serve their country in wartime and perform tasks never before done by women. Three of her Originals had died. Because of the nature of the assignment that brought them together, as ferry pilots they were always destined to go their separate ways.

On December 20, they would be history.

Chapter Twenty-three

The Hump

GENERAL C. R. SMITH was on his way to India for a one-month inspection tour the end of December. He needed information a general could not get.

The new supply route to India, called Crescent, was up and running. Crescent supplied the ATC's "Hump" airlift support flown from the U.S. to India's Assam Valley and on to the American and Chinese forces fighting in China. Smith needed to know—Was Crescent functioning well?

To find out, he needed the eyes and ears of a knowledgeable, observant individual. Nancy Love could do the job. She was no longer an active duty WASP, but she still was employed by the Ferrying Division. In order to do the job effectively, she could not accompany General Smith and his party in the general's C-54. She had to travel the Crescent route to India alone—undercover—and meet up with the general's party later.

Armed with security clearance and a passport and with orders in hand to fly halfway around the world, Nancy Love reported to the New York Aerial Port of Embarkation at La Guardia Field on December 27, 1944.

She boarded an ATC transport, destination Calcutta. She was sent under secret orders issued by General Nowland, "for purpose of

Nancy Love flies a B-25. *Courtesy: The Love family collection.*

coordinating Ferrying Division matters and upon completion thereof will return to Cincinnati, Ohio."

En route to India, Nancy noted several problems on the Crescent run: Passengers were delayed for lack of a reliable schedule and the Ferrying Division was getting a bad name. Planes failed to show up when expected. When they did arrive, many had mechanical problems. They were sent back to the States for repair rather than being sent on to India. Coordination and communications were sorely lacking.

In Calcutta, Nancy saw and talked to several former Ferrying Division pilots now flying C-46 cargo planes on scheduled runs for the North Africa or India-China Divisions. She learned that General Tunner's command was in dire need of radio operators and more pilots.

C-54 *Courtesy: National Museum of the US Air Force.*

Nancy visited the other ATC bases in the Assam Valley. She flew a staff B-25 to Delhi and to Agra. She logged sixteen hours in the cockpit over India. And, taking a short side trip, she visited the Taj Mahal.

Then came the opportunity to pilot General Smith's C-54 over the Hump route rather than go along as a passenger. This was not part of her assignment. Smith asked her to do it.

Nancy wrote little of this experience, but she dutifully recorded the flights in her logbook. From that information and stories she told her daughters, the flights on January 8 and 10, 1945, can be pieced together something like this:

> *January 8, 1945:* Cruising altitude was 16,000 feet, high enough to safely clear the 14,000-foot crests of the mountains on this route. The temperature aloft was on the far minus side of zero.

No freakish weather buffeted the plane and Japanese patrols were a thing of the past. When terraced rice paddies ringing the mountainsides came into view, Kunming, China, lay beyond. The flight pattern took them into a long low approach between craggy mountains—Mount Tali was 12,000 feet—and over Lake Tali, which sat at its base.

The descent into Kunming was hazardous. "Circle in a figure eight over the radio beacon and let down 500 feet at a time" were the standard instructions. This was to let the planes stacked in the landing pattern below land as their turn came. Elevation of the runway was 6,000 feet. Length of the runway also was 6,000 feet.

Most runways in wartime China were gravel, built by the toil of thousands of Chinese laborers. Native men and women crushed stone with hand-held hammers, carried the crushed stone by the basket load on their heads, dumped it out, and then spread it by hand on the leveled ground that was to be the runway. A massive roller, usually powered by the muscle of 200 workers rather than by steam, pressed the gravel flat so that airplanes could land on it.

In India, Nancy had watched elephants load fuel drums aboard transports. In Kunming, scores of Chinese coolies [cheap labor] flocked to the C-54 to unload that same cargo. That fuel would help the Chinese and U.S. armies in Kunming fight a little longer. Every flight over the Hump carried drums of precious aviation fuel in addition to other cargo and any passengers. Flight time from Calcutta was four hours, thirty minutes.

Nancy and the men found the high-altitude, wintery air refreshingly cold and crisp after the wretched humidity of Calcutta. They made their way to Operations and then to the mess hall. The traditional meal of fresh eggs fried in butter and lots of good hot coffee awaited them. Their party spent two nights in Kunming.

January 10, 1945: The morning they were to head back to Calcutta, Nancy and the other two pilots made the trip to Operations to get a weather briefing for the trip home.

Their route took them over rugged, ice-encrusted crags, the jungle and the gorges of the Mekong and Salween Rivers to Myitkyina where the two streams meet to form the Irrawaddy River that flows on to Mandalay and Rangoon. On this trip, they flew at 18,000 feet to cross the 15,000-foot-high peaks of the north-south Santsung Range that the American fliers had christened "the Rockpile."

The burned-out hulks of airplanes on the rocks below were mute testimony to why the Hump pilots referred to this route as "the aluminum trail." Before the end of the war, some 600 planes would go down trying to tame the Hump, with a loss of more than a thousand men—pilots, crews, and passengers.

Nancy and the men she flew with didn't dwell on what might have happened to anyone who survived the crashes. Neither desolate windswept crags nor the insect and reptile-infested jungle was a place a pilot would want his airplane to end up.

Why didn't Nancy write about the trip in later years? She professed not to be a writer. Nancy sought neither praise nor publicity. Her logbooks, her memories imparted to her three daughters, her comment in her trip report, and brief comments in later years are what we have.

Nancy receives the Air Medal from General Harold L. George. *Courtesy: The Love family collection.*

It is sad that we have only Nancy's logbooks and what she chose to tell her daughters. Her personal take on these precedent-breaking flights is forever lost to us.

She left India with General Smith and the crew January 29. The trip from Calcutta to Hickam Field in Honolulu took fifty flight hours. Nancy flew twenty of those hours.

Back in Cincinnati, she filed her report. With that, Nancy Love left behind, forever, a life she had never expected to lead. Although technically a civilian, she served as a military pilot for two and a half years during wartime. Her every move had been dictated by the needs of the WAFS, the WASP, the Ferrying Division, the Air Transport Command, and the U.S. Army Air Forces.

Her commanders, William H. Tunner, Robert M. Baker, and C.R. Smith, remained lifelong friends of Mr. and Mrs. Robert M. Love.

✈ ✈ ✈

On July 15, 1946, the U.S. Army Air Forces awarded medals to both Nancy and Bob for their service in World War II. They were the first husband and wife in Army history to be decorated simultaneously.

Bob received the Distinguished Service Medal. Nancy received the Air Medal along with a citation signed by President Harry Truman noting her "operational leadership in the successful training and assignment of over 300 qualified women fliers in the flying of advanced military aircraft."

Marky, Hannah, and Allie with their mom at the controls of the family Bonanza. *Courtesy the Love family collection.*

Epilogue

AFTER THE WAR, Nancy Love gave birth to three daughters: Hannah, Margaret ("Marky"), and Alice ("Allie.")

In late 1945, Bob Love was elected president of All American Aviation. The Loves settled in Washington, D.C., where the airline was headquartered. When All American became Allegheny Airlines, Bob was elected chairman of the board.

The Loves decided to move to Martha's Vineyard in 1952. Bob flew the family Bonanza to Washington on Mondays and returned to the island on Fridays, until he retired as Allegheny's board chair in 1954. The weekly commute was over. Year-round life on Martha's Vineyard became a Love family affair.

Nancy never aspired to hold another position of responsibility in aviation. Nor did she look for new fields to explore or conquer. She devoted herself to raising her three daughters. At thirty-three, she became a stay-at-home mom. She involved herself in her daughters and their needs and activities.

Because the entire island was their backyard, the girls had space in which to spread their wings as well as collect all the animals they wanted—dogs, cats and, of course, horses. All three Love girls had inherited their mother's love for horses.

The family loaded up the horses in the trailer every weekend, packed their gear, and hit the road for Mainland Massachusetts or New Hampshire or wherever the shows were held. They camped out at the horse shows. And then they drove home, dirty, smelly, tired, exhilarated. The more blue ribbons, the higher their spirits.

WASP Carolyn Cullen presents Nancy with a bouquet as the Love family leaves Martha's Vineyard to live in Florida. *Courtesy: The Love family collection.*

Bob was a lifelong sailor and Nancy, too, came to love sailing. It became a much larger part of their life than flying as the girls were growing up.

Every spring and fall, Nancy and Bob raced the family cutter against other sailing craft all over the East Coast. In the summer, the family took a leisurely cruise during which "we explore obscure little ports looking for adventure and the good company of other yachtsmen," Nancy once told a reporter.

Bob became the Vineyard's Harbor Master and he and Nancy ran Vineyard Yachts Inc. Nancy was the vice president of the corporation. "Dad didn't like running the day-to-day operation of a shipyard, so she did the office work and the paperwork," Allie said. Bob wanted to build boats.

Nancy considered writing the history of the WAFS, but her daughters say that she was too much of a perfectionist and destroyed any attempts she made. That is our loss.

Helen Mary Clark and family were next-door neighbors every summer and the two WAFS and their families played host to numerous lobster cookouts on the beach attended by the women pilots who had served with them.

Nancy continued to fly the Bonanza and later bought a single-engine, 100 horsepower Cessna 150 so that Carolyn Cullen, a WASP who lived on the island, could teach her girls how to fly.

"I won't teach you," Nancy told her daughters. She thought it better they learned from someone else. Both Hannah and Allie took to flying, but Marky tended to have motion sickness and did not. Nancy flew the Cessna, but after flying P-38s, B-17s and the C-54, the little two-seater was a bit tame.

When Allie left for her sophomore year in college, the Loves moved to Siesta Key, Florida.

Nancy battled cancer for several years and died on October 22, 1976, just when the WASP were gathering in Hot Springs, Arkansas, for their biennial reunion.

Earlier in October, the WASP had named Nancy Love "1976 Woman of the Year." WASP President Bee Haydu called Marky to tell her. They hoped Nancy could attend the upcoming reunion, but by then the doctors had told the Love family her illness was terminal.

Marky called Bee in Hot Springs to tell her of Nancy's passing. Bee vividly recalls having to make that sad announcement to the gathering.

Nancy received many posthumous honors. Possibly the greatest was induction into the National Aviation Hall of Fame in Dayton, Ohio, July 16, 2005. She was the ninth woman so honored in the first thirty-eight years of the Hall of Fame's existence. She followed

Air Transport Command Civilian Wings worn by the WAFS. *Courtesy: Author's Personal Collection. Photo by Joe Weingarten.*

Amelia Earhart, Anne Morrow Lindbergh, Jacqueline Cochran, Olive Ann Beech, Louise Thaden, Ruth Nichols, Harriet Quimby, and Patti Wagstaff.

Since 2005, Geraldyn "Jerrie" Cobb, Bessie Coleman, Eileen Collins, Evelyn Bryan Johnson, Sally Ride, Betty Skelton, and Emily Howell Warner have followed Nancy onto that distinguished list.

Nancy Love has taken her well-deserved place among aviation's greats.

Flying High

A SHORT BIOGRAPHY OF NANCY appeared in the October 1943 issue of *Calling All Girls*. The publisher of the magazine, which was in print from 1941 to 1949, was The Parents' Magazine Press Division of The Parents' Institute, Inc., with offices in Chicago and New York City. The Executive Editor was Frances Ullmann; the Art Editor was Ralph O. Ellsworth.

A comic strip about a famous woman or girl of the time was featured in each issue. A copy sold for ten cents. Among the advisory editors listed in the October 1943 issue are well-known 1940s-era names, such as Shirley Temple, movie star; Sonja Henie, world-famous ice skater; and Osa Johnson, jungle explorer.

Nancy's daughters own a copy of the magazine, and it is part of the Nancy Harkness Love collection of papers.

Aircraft Flown by Nancy during World War II

NANCY FLEW TWENTY-ONE different military aircraft during the war.

L4-B Piper "Grasshopper"—single Continental engine, 65 horsepower (hp). Maximum speed, 85 mph; cruising speed, 75 mph; range 190 miles; service ceiling, 9,300 feet.

PT-19—Fairchild—single Ranger engine, 175 hp. Maximum speed, 124 mph; cruising speed, 106 mph; range, 480 miles; service ceiling, 16,000. Open-cockpit, low wing.

BT-13—Vultee "Valiant" (also known as the Vultee Vibrator): single Pratt & Whitney engine, 450 hp. Maximum speed, 155 mph; cruising speed, 130 mph; range 880 miles; service ceiling, 19,400 feet.

BT-15—450-hp Vultee basic trainer, but with a Wright rather than a Pratt & Whitney engine.

AT-6 (BC-1)—North American "Texan" C model—single 600-hp Pratt & Whitney engine; Maximum speed 206 mph; cruising speed 145 mph; range 1,000 miles with drop tank; service ceiling, 23,200 feet.

UC-43—Beech, 1 Pratt & Whitney, Jacobs or Wright engine, most were 450 hp; top speed 180-200 mph.

UC-78—Cessna, 2 Jacobs engines, 225 hp each, top speed 175 mph.

C-36—Lockheed twin-engine, Pratt & Whitney, 450 hp each.

C-45—Beech, 2 Pratt & Whitney engines, 450 hp each; top speed 218 mph.

C-47—Douglas "Skytrain": twin Pratt & Whitney engines, 1,200 hp each. Maximum speed, 232 mph; cruising speed, 175 mph; range, 1,513 miles; service ceiling, 24,450. The military version of the civilian DC-3 airliner.

C-53—Douglas: twin 1,200 hp. Maximum speed 212 mph.

C-54—Douglas "Skymaster": four Pratt & Whitney engines, 1,450 hp each. Maximum speed, 300 mph; cruising speed, 245 mph; range, 3,900 miles; service ceiling, 30,000 feet.

C-60—Lockheed "Lodestar": A model—twin Wright engines, 1,200 hp each. Maximum speed 257 mph; cruising speed, 232 mph; range, 1,700 miles; service ceiling, 25,000 feet.

C-73—Boeing, two Pratt & Whitney engines, 600 hp each; top speed 200 mph.

B-17—Boeing "Flying Fortress": four Wright Cyclone engines, 1,200 hp each. Maximum speed, 300 mph; cruising speed, 170 mph; range, 1,850 miles; service ceiling, 35,000 feet. Carried a 6,000-pound bomb load.

B-24—Liberator [Nancy flew a Ford-built model] Four Pratt & Whitney engines, 1,200 hp each.

B-25—North American "Mitchell" twin Wright engines, 1700 hp each. Maximum speed, 275 mph; cruising speed, 230 mph; range, 1,200 miles; service ceiling, 25,000 miles. Carried 5,000-pound bomb load.

A-20 (DB-7)—Douglas "Havoc" twin Wright engines, 1600 hp each. Maximum speed 317 mph; cruising speed 230 mph; range of 1,025 miles; service ceiling, 25,000 feet.

A-24—Douglas "Dauntless" single Wright engine, 1,000 hp. Maximum speed, 254 mph; range, 1,100 miles; service ceiling, 24,300 feet.

P-38—Lockheed "Lightning" L model—two Allison engines, 1,475 hp each. Maximum speed 414 mph; cruising speed, 275 mph; range 1,100 miles; service ceiling, 40,000 feet. Tricycle gear as opposed to a tail dragger.

P-51—North American "Mustang" C model—single Packard-built Rolls-Royce "Merlin" engine, 1,695 hp. Maximum speed, 425 mph; cruising speed, 275 mph; range 1,000 miles; service ceiling, 41,900 feet.

Awards and Honors

July 15, 1946—Received Air Medal presented by President Truman, in recognition of her wartime performance as leader of 303 women ferry pilots.

October 23, 1976—Designated Woman of the Year, 1976, by the WASP organization the Order of Fifinella.

June 1979—Inducted into the International Forest of Friendship, Atchison, Kansas—Amelia Earhart's birthplace.

May 1980—The Houghton, Michigan, Chapter # 638 of the Experimental Aircraft Association (EAA) changed its name to the Nancy Harkness Love Memorial Chapter.

October 13, 1989—Inducted into the Michigan Aviation Hall of Fame, Kalamazoo. Award presented by friend and fellow member of the Ninety-Nines, Alice Hammond, and accepted by Hannah Love Robinson.

November 1996—Inducted into the Airlift/Tanker Hall of Fame.

November 1, 1997—Inducted into the Michigan Women's Hall of Fame, Lansing. Accepted by Nancy Walters, Michigan Ninety-Nine.

March 22, 2003—Selected as one of the 100 Most Influential Women in Aviation and Aerospace since the Wright brothers flew at Kitty Hawk, December 17, 1903. The occasion was the Women In Aviation International 2003 celebration of the Centennial of Powered Flight. WAFS Betty Gillies and Cornelia Fort were included in that number as was Jackie Cochran.

July 16, 2005—Inducted into the National Aviation Hall of Fame, The Museum of the United States Air Force in Dayton, Ohio.

Glossary and Acronyms

AAB—Army Air Base

AAF—Army Air Forces

AT—Advanced training aircraft flown in the third stage of Army flight instruction.

ATA—Air Transport Auxiliary (to the British Royal Air Force—see RAF)

ATC—Air Transport Command

BOQ—Bachelor Officer Quarters

BT—Basic training aircraft flown in the second stage of Army flight instruction.

CAA—Civil Aeronautics Authority (1938-1940); Civil Aeronautics Administration (1940-1958)

CAP—Civil Air Patrol

Ceiling—Vertical distance from ground to cloud cover

CO—Commanding Officer

Commercial License—A federal certificate that allowed a pilot to carry passengers for hire or to haul freight.

Control Tower—Tower at an airfield with air traffic controllers who stay in radio contact with pilots in the area, giving them orders until the plane leaves the area or turns off onto the taxiway and is under ground control via radioed orders.

CPT Program—Civilian Pilot Training, a federal program that subsidized individuals learning to fly 1939-1941.

HQ—Headquarters

Instrument Conditions—When there is no visible horizon or when the ceiling is lower than allowable for visual flying.

Private License—A federal license earned by a pilot who has demonstrated sufficient skills to be allowed to carry passengers, but not for hire.

PT—Primary trainer, flown in the first stage of Army flight instruction training in WWII.

RAF—Royal Air Force

RON—Remain Over Night

Stick—A control device usually found in single-engine aircraft. It operates the ailerons and the elevators.

Transition—Instructing a pilot on how to fly an aircraft in which the pilot lacks experience.

WAC—Women's Army Corps

WAFS—Women's Auxiliary Ferrying Squadron

WASP—Women Airforce Service Pilots

WFTD—Women's Flying Training Detachment

WTS—War Training Service (followed CPT, 1941-1944)

Timeline

February 14, 1914 – Hannah Lincoln "Nancy" Harkness born in Houghton, Michigan.

November 7, 1930 – Earned Private Pilot Certificate # 17797 at age sixteen.

April 25, 1932 – Earned Limited Commercial License at age eighteen.

August 13, 1933 – Earned Transport License at age nineteen.

1934–1936 – Worked as a charter pilot for Boston-based Inter City Aviation.

1935 – Worked for the National Airmarking Program, Bureau of Air Commerce.

January 11, 1936 – Married Robert MacLure Love.

1937 – Worked for the National Airmarking Program, Bureau of Air Commerce.

1937 – Worked as a demonstration pilot for the experimental tricycle gear safety plane, the Hammond Y Plane.

1937-1938 – Worked as a demonstration pilot for the Gwinn Aircar Co. Aircar.

1938-1941 – Again worked as a charter pilot for Inter City Aviation.

September 1, 1939 – Germany invaded Poland and World War II began in Europe.

May 21, 1940 – Nancy Love proposed the use of civilian women pilots to ferry military aircraft, before the United States entered World War II.

December 7, 1941 – Japanese aircraft attacked the U.S. Naval Fleet at Pearl Harbor. The United States entered World War II.

March-June 1942 – Operations manager with Domestic Wing of the Ferrying Command, renamed the Ferrying Division, Air Transport Command.

Summer 1942 – Established, with Col. William H. Tunner, the Women's Auxiliary Ferrying Squadron (WAFS), Ferrying Division, Air Transport Command, U.S. Army Air Forces.

September 10, 1942 – Appointed Leader of the Women's Auxiliary Ferrying Squadron (WAFS), Ferrying Division, ATC, USAAF.

February 27, 1943 – First woman to fly the P-51 Mustang fighter aircraft. Over the next 24 months, she flew the B-25 Mitchell, B-17 Flying Fortress, P-38 Lightning, C-47 Skytrain, and C-54 Skymaster.

July 5, 1943 – Named WAFS Executive on staff of the commander of the Ferrying Division.

August 1943 – Named WASP Executive on staff of the commander of the Ferrying Division. Exercised staff supervision over all WASP ferrying squadrons in the ATC.

December 20, 1944 – WASP were deactivated.

January 1945 – Conducted special air operations and flight safety assessment for the Air Transport Command in India and China.

August 14, 1945 – VJ Day, World War II ended.

August 1947 – Gave birth to Hannah Lincoln Love in Wilmington, Delaware.

1948 – Commissioned a Lt. Colonel in the United States Air Force Reserve for her role as a founder of the women pilot program that evolved within the wartime Army Air Forces. Later withdrawn because she had minor children at home.

March 1949 – Gave birth to Margaret Campbell "Marky" Love, in Alexandria, Virginia.

November 1951 – Gave birth to Alice Harkness "Allie" Love, in Alexandria, Virginia.

April 1952 – The Loves moved to Martha's Vineyard, Massachusetts.

Fall 1970 – Nancy and Bob moved to Sarasota, Florida.

1974 – Nancy was diagnosed with breast cancer.

October 22, 1976 – Nancy died in Sarasota, Florida.

Bibliography

Published Works

Arnold, H.H. *Global Mission*. Blue Ridge Summit, Pennsylvania: Military Classics Series, TAB Books Inc., Harper & Row Publishers, 1949.

Bartels, Diane Ruth Armour. *Sharpie: The Life Story of Evelyn Sharp*. Lincoln, Nebraska: Dageforde Publishing, 1996.

Bunting, Edward, et al., editors. *World War II Day by Day*. London: Dorling Kindersley Limited, 2001.

Churchill, Jan. *On Wings to War: Teresa James, Aviator*. Manhattan, Kansas: Sunflower University Press, 1992.

Cochran, Jacqueline and Maryann Bucknum Brinley. *Jackie Cochran: The Autobiography of the Greatest Woman Pilot in Aviation History*. New York: Bantam Books, 1987.

Cochran, Jacqueline. *The Stars at Noon*. An Atlantic Monthly Press Book, Boston: Little, Brown and Company, 1954.

Cole, Jean Hascall. *Women Pilots of World War II*. Salt Lake City: University of Utah Press, 1992.

Constein, Carl Frey. *Born to Fly the Hump, A WWII Memoir*. Shawnee Mission, Kansas: Johnson County Library, 2000.

Douglas, Deborah G. *American Women and Flight since 1940*. Lexington: University Press of Kentucky, 2004.

Fahey, James C., author and editor. *U.S. Army Aircraft (Heavier Than Air) 1908-1946*. New York: Ships and Aircraft, 1946.

Gott, Kay. *Women In Pursuit*. Self Published, 1993.

Granger, Byrd Howell. *On Final Approach: The Women Airforce Service Pilots of W.W.II*. Scottsdale, Arizona: Falconer Publishing Company, 1991.

Hodgson, Marion Stegeman. *Winning My Wings*. Albany, Texas: Bright Sky Press, 1996.

Holm, Jeanne. *Women in the Military: An Unfinished Revolution*. Novato, California: Presidio Press, 1982, revised 1992.

Keil, Sally Van Wagenen. *Those Wonderful Women In Their Flying Machines: The Unknown Heroines of World War II*. New York: Four Directions Press, 1979, 1990.

La Farge, Oliver. *The Eagle in the Egg*. Boston: Houghton Mifflin Company, Riverside Press Cambridge, 1949.

Lewis, W. David and William F. Trimble. *The Airway to Everywhere: A History of All American Aviation, 1937-1953*. Pittsburgh: University of Pittsburgh Press, 1988.

Makanna, Philip and Jeffrey Ethell. *Ghosts: Vintage Aircraft of World War II*. Charlottesville, Virginia: Thomasson-Grant, Inc., 1987.

Matz, Onas P. *History of the 2nd Ferrying Group, Ferrying Division, Air Transport Command*. Seattle, Washington: Modet Enterprises, Inc., 1993. Sponsored by the Wilmington Warrior Association.

Merryman, Molly. *Clipped Wings, The Rise and Fall of the Women Airforce Service Pilots (WASPs) of World War II*. New York and London: New York University Press, 1998.

Moser, Don, et al., editors. *China-Burma-India*. Alexandria, Virginia: World War II—Time-Life Books, 1978.

Rich, Doris L. *Jackie Cochran: Pilot in the Fastest Lane*. Gainesville: University Press of Florida, 2007.

Rickman, Sarah Byrn. *The Originals: The Women's Auxiliary Ferrying Squadron of World War II*. Sarasota, Florida: Disc-Us Books, Inc., 2001.

Scharr, Adela Riek. *Sisters in the Sky*, Volumes I and II. St. Louis: Patrice Press, 1986.

Seymour, Dawn, Clarice I. Bergemann, Jeannette J. Jenkins, and Mary Ellen Keil. *In Memoriam Thirty-eight American Women Pilots*. Denton, Texas: Texas Woman's University Press, no year given.

Simbeck, Rob. *Daughter of the Air: The Brief Soaring Life of Cornelia Fort*. New York: Atlantic Monthly Press, 1999.

Strickland, Patricia. *The Putt-Putt Air Force: The Story of The Civilian Pilot Training Program and The War Training Service (1939-1944)*. Department of Transportation, Federal Aviation Administration, Aviation Education Staff, GA-20-84.

Thaden, Louise. *High, Wide and Frightened*. New York: Air Facts Press, 1973.

————. *The Concise Columbia Encyclopedia*. New York, Avon Books, a division of The Hearst Corporation, 1983.

Treadwell, Mattie E. *The Women's Army Corps*. Washington, D.C.: Office of the Chief of Military History, Department of the Army, 1954—copyright 1953.

Tunner, William H. and Booton Herndon. *Over the Hump: The Story of General William H. Tunner, the Man Who Moved Anything, Anywhere, Anytime*. New York: Duell, Sloan and Pearce, 1964.

————. United States Air Force Museum, Aircraft Brochure featuring more than 175 aircraft of the U.S. Aircraft Museum, with aircraft photos, text, and specifications, Newly Revised Edition, 2003.

Verges, Marianne. *On Silver Wings*. New York: Ballantine Books, 1991.

Ware, Susan, editor. *Notable American Women, A Biographical Dictionary Completing the Twentieth Century*. Cambridge, Massachusetts: The Belknap Press of Harvard University Press, 2004.

Warren, Margaret Thomas. *Taking Off*. Worcestershire, England: Images Publishing, Malvern Ltd., 1993.

Government Historical Studies, WWII

"History of the Air Transport Command, Women Pilots in the Air Transport Command," prepared by the Historical Branch, Intelligence and Security Division, Headquarters, Air Transport Command in accordance with ATC Regulation 20-20, AAF Regulation 20-8, and AR 345-105, as amended. Author is Lt. Col. Oliver LaFarge, official historian for the Air Transport Command. This is the accepted history on the women ferry pilots of the ATC.

"History of the Air Transport Command: Women Pilots in the Air Transport Command." Historical data prepared by the Historical Branch, Intelligence and Security Division, Headquarters, Air Transport Command in accordance with ATC Regulation 20-20, AAF Regulation 20-8, and AR 345-105, as amended. WASP Archival Collection, Texas Woman's University Library, Denton, Texas.

Rhodes, Jeffrey P. *Chronology: The Army Air Corps to World War II.* Air Force History Support Office. Material courtesy *Air Force* magazine, December 1993.

"Women Pilots in the Ferrying Division, Air Transport Command." A history written in accordance with AAF Regulation No. 20-8 and AAF Letter 40-34; unpublished. Capt. Walter J. Marx. The Nancy Harkness Love private collection. A copy is also in the author's files.

"Women Pilots AAF, 1941-1944." Army Air Forces Historical Studies: No. 55. March 1946. This document (an abstract) is part of the WASP Archival Collection, Texas Woman's University Library, Denton, Texas. It also is part of the Jacqueline Cochran Collection, Dwight D. Eisenhower Presidential Library, Abilene, Kansas. A shortened version of this history is commonly referred to as "Number 55."

Unpublished Sources

Memoir
Delphine Bohn. "Catch a Shooting Star"—copies in hands of the author and the WASP Archives, Texas Woman's University.

Personal Papers

Dwight D. Eisenhower Presidential Library
Jacqueline Cochran Collection

International Women's Air and Space Museum Collections
Betty Huyler Gillies
Nancy Harkness Love

U.S. Air Force Museum Library
Pat Pateman Collection

WASP Archives, Texas Woman's University Collections
Nancy Harkness Love

Video Sources

Fly Girls. A Silverlining Productions Film for *The American Experience*, PBS, Boston: WGBH Educational Foundation, 2000. Written, produced and directed by Laurel Ladevich.

Flying the Hump: The China Airlift. Commemorative Edition, Volume 2. Seattle, Memory Maker Productions Inc., 1990.

Personal Interviews

Nancy Batson Crews—WAFS

Iris Cummings Critchell—WASP

Betty Huyler Gillies (WAFS)—oral history interview done by Dawn Letson of Texas Woman's University

Barbara Jane (BJ) Erickson London—WAFS

Alice Harkness and Margaret Campbell Love and Hannah Love Robinson—daughters of WAFS Nancy Harkness Love

Florene Miller Watson—WAFS

In addition, the author has conducted personal interviews with approximately 60 WASP as part of the WASP Archives Oral History project, Texas Woman's University.

Internet Sources

Airlift/Tanker Association Hall of Fame: www.atalink.org/hallfame/c.r.smith.html.

Civilian Pilot Training Program; www.centennialofflight.gov/essay/GENERAL_AVIATION/civilian_pilot_training/GA20.htm

Harmon Trophy, source: http://en.wikipedia.org/wiki/Harmon_Trophy

Houghton, Michigan, http://history.cityofhoughton.com/

National Postal Museum Web site: www.postalmuseum.si.edu/resources/6a2w_airpickup.html

North American Aviation, history (P-51)—www.boeing.com/company/offices/history/bna/p51

The P-38 National Association and Museum—http://p38assn.org/museum.htm

Acknowledgments

Nancy Love, WASP Pilot, a biography for Young Adult readers, is published thanks to the help, encouragement, and cooperation of several people.

My grateful thanks go to:

Allie Love, Marky Love and Hannah Love Robinson, Nancy Love's daughters who were invaluable to me in the writing of my first biography about their mother, *Nancy Love and the WASP Ferry Pilots of World War II*, published 2008 by the University of North Texas Press. Allie has provided additional assistance with this new volume.

Ron Chrisman, the University of North Texas Press, my editor for the 2008 biography of Nancy. Ron graciously approved and granted permission for me to base the new Young Adult volume on the research for, and the content of, my first Love biography.

Kimberly Johnson and her staff, Texas Woman's University, the WASP Archive, without whose help, cooperation and friendship this book could not have seen light of day.

Carol Cain, my buddy at the WASP WWII Museum in Sweetwater, who faithfully stocks my books in their Gift Shop!

Women in Aviation, International, for their ongoing interest and support.

Doris Baker, my editor and publisher from Filter Press, who believed in my ability to write for young women and was willing to publish my efforts. This is our second book together.

My friends Jacque Boyd and Nancy Jurka, the first to convince me to tell the WASP stories for today's young women.

About the Author

Nancy Love: WASP Pilot is Sarah Byrn Rickman's ninth book about the WASP of WWII. It is her second book aimed at introducing young readers to the gutsy women who paved the way for today's women military pilots.

Sarah also serves as editor of the *WASP News*, the official newsletter for the WASP Archives, located at the Texas Woman's University Library, Denton, Texas.

Contact the author through her web site: www.sarahbyrnrickman.com.

Also by Sarah Byrn Rickman

Nonfiction

- *BJ ERICKSON: WASP PILOT*
  Filter Press, Palmer Lake, CO, 2018 (Y/A biography)
- *FINDING DOROTHY SCOTT: Letters of a WASP Pilot*
  Texas Tech University Press, 2016 (biography)
- *WASP OF THE FERRY COMMAND: Women Pilots, Uncommon Deeds*
  University of North Texas Press, 2016
- *NANCY BATSON CREWS: Alabama's First Lady of Flight*
  University of Alabama Press, 2009 (biography)
- *NANCY LOVE and the WASP FERRY PILOTS OF WORLD WAR II*
  University of North Texas Press, 2008 (biography)
- *THE ORIGINALS: The Women's Auxiliary Ferrying Squadron of World War II*
  Disc-Us Books, Inc., Sarasota, FL, 2001
  Second edition, Braughler Books, Springboro, OH, 2017

Fiction

- *FLIGHT FROM FEAR*
  Disc-Us Books, Inc., Sarasota, FL, 2002
- *FLIGHT TO DESTINY, A WASP Novel*
  Greyden Press, Dayton, OH, 2014
  Second edition, Braughler Books, Springboro, OH, 2017